Advancing Studies in Religion
SERIES EDITOR: Sarah Wilkins-Laflamme

Advancing Studies in Religion catalyzes and provokes original research in the study of religion with a critical edge. The series advances the study of religion in method and theory, textual interpretation, theological studies, and the understanding of lived religious experience. Rooted in the long and diverse traditions of the study of religion in Canada, the series demonstrates awareness of the complex genealogy of religion as a category and as a discipline. ASR welcomes submissions from authors researching religion in varied contexts and with diverse methodologies.

The series is sponsored by the Canadian Corporation for Studies in Religion whose constituent societies include the Canadian Society of Biblical Studies, Canadian Society for the Study of Religion, Canadian Society of Patristic Studies, Canadian Theological Society, Société canadienne de théologie, and Société québécoise pour l'étude de la religion.

The Journey Presses On

Pope Francis's Apology to Residential School Survivors in Canada

EDITED BY

DORIS M. KIESER

AND

JANE BARTER

McGill-Queen's University Press

Montreal & Kingston

ISBN 978-0-2280-2896-3 (cloth)
ISBN 978-0-2280-2983-0 (ePDF)
ISBN 978-0-2280-2914-4 (ePUB)

Legal deposit third quarter 2026
Bibliothèque et Archives nationales du Québec

Printed in Canada on acid-free paper that is 100% ancient-forest-free, containing 100% sustainable, recycled fibre, and processed chlorine-free.

This book has been published with the help of a grant from the Federation for the Humanities and Social Sciences, through the Scholarly Book Awards, using funds provided by the Social Sciences and Humanities Research Council of Canada.

Funded by the Government of Canada | Financé par le gouvernement du Canada | Canada | Canada Council for the Arts | Conseil des arts du Canada

We acknowledge the support of the Canada Council for the Arts.
Nous remercions le Conseil des arts du Canada de son soutien.

McGill-Queen's University Press in Montreal is on land which long served as a site of meeting and exchange amongst Indigenous Peoples, including the Haudenosaunee and Anishinabeg nations. In Kingston it is situated on the territory of the Haudenosaunee and Anishinaabek. We acknowledge and thank the diverse Indigenous Peoples whose footsteps have marked these territories on which peoples of the world now gather.

Library and Archives Canada Cataloguing in Publication

Title: The journey presses on : Pope Francis's apology to residential school survivors in Canada / edited by Doris M. Kieser and Jane Barter.
Names: Kieser, Doris M., editor. | Barter, Jane, editor.
Series: Advancing studies in religion ; 20.
Description: Series statement: Advancing studies in religion ; 20 | Includes bibliographical references and index.
Identifiers: Canadiana (print) 20260149829 | Canadiana (ebook) 20260157910 | ISBN 9780228028963 (cloth) | ISBN 9780228029144 (EPUB) | ISBN 9780228029830 (PDF)
Subjects: CSH: Indigenous peoples—Canada—Residential schools. | LCSH: Francis, Pope, 1936-2025—Travel—Canada. | LCSH: Catholic Church—Canada—History. | LCSH: Papal visits—Canada. | LCSH: Reconciliation—Religious aspects—Catholic Church. | LCSH: Colonization—Religious aspects—Catholic Church.
Classification: LCC E96.5 .J68 2026 | DDC 371.829/97071—dc23

This book was designed and typeset by oneonone in Adobe Garamond 11/14.
Copyediting by Robert Lewis.

McGill-Queen's University Press
Suite 1720, 1010 Sherbrooke St West, Montreal, QC, H3A 2R7

Authorized safety representative in the EU: Mare Nostrum Group BV, Doelen 72, 4831 GR Breda, the Netherlands, gpsr@mare-nostrum.co.uk

Contents

The Journey Presses On

Introduction

Doris M. Kieser and Jane Barter

WRESTLING WITH THE APOLOGIES: PERSONAL REFLECTIONS

After the first papal apology to the survivors of Canada's Indian residential schools, delivered to an Indigenous delegation that visited Rome from 28 March to 1 April 2022, we began our work of unpacking the pope's apology and the responses that this early encounter elicited. The natural place for us to begin such work was the annual meeting of the Canadian Theological Society, which took place online in late May of that year. Still grappling with the Covid-19 pandemic, we watched the apology made in Rome together via Zoom, and our initial panel was marked by the optimism that many of us felt about Pope Francis, a pope renowned for his solidarity with the oppressed and the marginalized. We hoped that the pope would help to move the Canadian Catholic Church finally toward a meaningful expression of repentance and reconciliation. By the time the Canadian Theological Society met again – this time in person in the spring of 2023 – almost a year had passed since the apology in Rome and the pope's subsequent visit to Canada in July 2022. Pope Francis's visit had inspired a wealth of commentary, especially by Indigenous scholars, intellectuals, and activists, who prophetically spoke out about the limitations and missed opportunities of the pope's apologies in Canada: the failure to apologize specifically for the church's responsibility for the residential schools and for the sexual abuse that happened there, as well as the failure to address the abiding legacy of the Doctrine of Discovery.

When we convened a second panel on the papal apologies at the Canadian Theological Society, the tenor of our conversations was palpably different. Pope Francis had visited Canada and apologized to the survivors of the residential schools. But many of the respondents were less hopeful than during the initial round of conversations. This change had to do primarily with what the pope had not said. Many experienced the visit as a missed opportunity for Pope Francis to offer a truly decolonial vision, one that would implicate the church as at least a colonial agent, if not architect.

We knew then that we had to move our prior work, which had been published as a special symposium in the *Journal of Moral Theology*, outward from a primarily Catholic audience. We understood that this apology had implications far beyond the Catholic world in North America; indeed, it was significant to Indigenous peoples worldwide who were wrestling with the legacy of colonialism, and it also had far-reaching political implications in Canada. Moreover, we knew that it was important to publish this volume in the Canadian context in order to ensure its accessibility to all survivors, elders, knowledge keepers, and their families across Turtle Island.

This volume specifically addresses Pope Francis's visit to Canada following his apology on 1 April 2022 to the Indigenous delegation in Rome. The ensuing diverse discussion captures reflections from Indigenous and non-Indigenous responders to the pope's apology to Indigenous peoples in Canada along a spectrum of experience. In the varied reflections, we witness responses both to the apology itself and to the long process by which it came to pass. At the Canadian Theological Society meeting and conference in May 2023, Dr Christine Jamieson (Concordia University),

Dr Niigaan Sinclair (University of Manitoba), Dr Chantal Fiola (University of Winnipeg), Dr Annie Selak (Georgetown University), Dr Timothy Harvie (St Mary's University), and Dr Darren Dias (University of St Michael's College and the Toronto School of Theology) offered initial perceptions of the papal apologies, and their insights are expanded upon here. Also included in this collection are the reflections of Dr Jeremy M. Bergen (Conrad Grebel University College) and of Archbishop Donald Bolen (Catholic Archdiocese of Regina), developed from their initial responses to the apologies in May 2022 and formulated from within their own history and in accord with their own hopes. The insights shared by these authors shed light on the reception of Pope Francis's two apologetic and penitential moments.

Our own positionalities as editors of such a work reflect some of the ambivalence that is felt about the papal visit. We are both settler Canadians of European descent. Doris is a Catholic theologian, and Jane is an Anglican, with both of us coming from ecclesial homes that are deeply implicated in the colonial project in Canada as institutions that ran the residential schools. We are theologians who have spent most of our careers in western Canada – Alberta and Manitoba respectively – during a period of profound Indigenous resurgence that has affected and inspired our own theological projects. It is a humbling thing to witness this resurgence, which questions the very foundations of theology and calls us to resist "settler moves to innocence."[1] We hope that this volume responds faithfully to such a prophetic call.

In preparing this book, we sought to centre Indigenous writers, yet this task is complex, for Indigenous scholars are often overburdened by requests to contribute their expertise to such projects. We are therefore deeply grateful to Christine Jamieson, Chantal Fiola, and Niigaan Sinclair for offering their important contributions to this volume. We also sought out experts on ecclesial apologies, namely Jeremy M. Bergen and Annie Selak, who helped to contextualize this apology within both an ecumenical and a Catholic frame. Finally, we wanted to situate this apology within the broader context of Pope Francis's theological and political vision. We are thus deeply grateful to Donald Bolen, Timothy

Harvie, and Darren Dias for helping to adumbrate this dimension of the apology, both as Francis scholars and, in the case of Bolen and Dias, as individuals who were actively engaged in the visit itself – Bolen as one of the key organizers of the visit and Dias as a regular commentator with the press during the visit.

RECOVERING GRAVESITES: A ROMAN CATHOLIC LEGACY

The history of Indian residential schools in Canada hangs heavily across the Catholic Church and beyond. Although the Canadian federal government was the original architect of the plan to assimilate Indigenous Peoples, many Christian churches participated in the institutionalization of First Nations, Métis, and Inuit children who were forcibly removed from their homes and communities. The Roman Catholic Church in Canada operated many of the schools, from coast to coast to coast, and has been the focus of those seeking accountability for the unmarked gravesites detected on church properties. In this context, the impetus for this collection was the May 2021 globally broken news of 215 unmarked graves detected at the site of the former Kamloops Indian Residential School in British Columbia. Located on the traditional territory of the Tk'emlúps te Secwépemc people, the school housed around 500 students at its peak. The unmarked graves are believed to hold Indigenous children who died while at the school.[2] Like many others across Canada, the school was run by the Missionary Oblates of Mary Immaculate, a Roman Catholic religious order, which operated the school from 1893 to 1969, when it was taken over by the federal government.[3] It remained open until 1978.

The detection of the gravesites using ground-penetrating radar, although shocking to all, was not surprising to Indigenous elders, knowledge keepers, and the survivors of residential schools and their families across Canada. Among the ninety-four *Calls to Action* (2015) of the Truth and Reconciliation Commission of Canada (TRC), calls 71 to 76 directly identify the fact of the missing children and recommend that key institutions rectify their lack of transparency regarding burial information.[4] These six calls are directed at the Christian churches and religious orders involved in running the residential schools, at the various levels of government keeping statistical and archival records of the residential school system, and at the federal government. These records were not made available to the TRC prior to the May 2021 discovery of the gravesites.

Tk'emlúps te Secwépamc's discovery of gravesites was the first of many across the country. Over the course of the following years, approximately 2,671 additional graves have been identified at the sites of former Indian residential schools in provinces and territories across Turtle Island.[5] Many more are likely to follow. In June 2022, some seven years after the TRC published its recommendations, the Ministry of Justice and the Office of the Attorney General of Canada responded to the detection of the gravesites by establishing the Office of the Independent Special Interlocutor for Missing Children and Unmarked Graves and Burial Sites Associated with Indian Residential Schools, led by Kimberly Murray.[6] The mandate of the independent special interlocutor is as follows:

> The Special Interlocutor will identify needed measures and make recommendations for a new federal legal framework to ensure the respectful and culturally appropriate treatment of unmarked graves and burial sites of children at former Indian Residential Schools and associated institutions.
>
> This will be done in close collaboration with First Nations, Inuit and Métis governments, representative organizations, communities, Survivors and families, the federal, provincial, and territorial governments and other relevant institutions such as church entities and record holders.
>
> The Special Interlocutor will function independently and impartially, in a non-partisan and transparent manner to achieve the objectives of her mandate.[7]

The interim report of the special independent interlocutor, *Sacred Responsibility: Searching for the Missing Children and Unmarked Burials*

(2023), and the follow-up historical report, *Sites of Truth, Sites of Conscience: Unmarked Burials and Mass Graves of Missing and Disappeared Indigenous Children in Canada* (2024), outline the history, challenges, possibilities for recovery, and continuing identification of gravesites across Turtle Island.[8] The special interlocutor is charged with the responsibility to recommend improvements to the Canadian legal processes in place "to identify and protect the unmarked graves and burial sites associated with former Indian Residential Schools across the country." Ultimately, "recommendations for a new federal framework will be made to ensure that the bodies and Spirits of the children are treated with honour, respect and dignity."[9] Given Canadian cultural developments in understanding the nature and extent of the abuses at Indian residential schools, the loss of lives, and the lack of historical transparency with records of these events, the whole church is now aware of and called to respond in solidarity with First Nations, Métis, and Inuit people across the land.

HISTORY AND TRUTH AND RECONCILIATION

Included in the TRC's *Calls to Action* was call 58's demand for an apology from the Catholic Church:

> We call upon the Pope to issue an apology to Survivors, their families, and communities for the Roman Catholic Church's role in the spiritual, cultural, emotional, physical, and sexual abuse of First Nations, Inuit, and Métis children in Catholic-run residential schools. We call for that apology to be similar to the 2010 apology issued to Irish victims of abuse and to occur within one year of the issuing of this Report and to be delivered by the Pope in Canada.[10]

With the initial recovery of gravesites came renewed calls for a papal apology on Indigenous Canadian soil. Pope Benedict XVI had some time ago "expressed his sorrow at the anguish caused by the deplorable conduct of some members of the Church and he offered his sympathy and prayerful solidarity," in a statement issued by the Holy See Press Office following a private audience with Indigenous and church leaders in Rome in 2009.[11] These words were subsequently not understood as an adequate papal apology.[12]

Although Pope Francis's apologies in 2022 were long delayed following the TRC's *Calls to Action*, numerous previous apologies from various Catholic entities were made to Indigenous peoples in Canada, including the Oblate Conference of Canada's initial "An Apology to the First Nations of Canada" (1991), issued on behalf of the Missionary Oblates of Mary Immaculate, and the Canadian Religious Conference's "Statement on Behalf of Congregations of Women Religious Involved in the Indian Residential Schools of Canada" (2009).[13] Apologies in the form of letters, published statements, verbal addresses, and public homilies were also extended by various bishops and bishops' groups: Archbishop Austin E. Burke of Halifax, Nova Scotia (1992), Archbishop Gerald Pettipas of Grouard-McLennan, Alberta (2008), Bishop Albert LeGatt of Saskatoon, Saskatchewan (2008), Archbishop Sylvain Lavoie of Keewatin–Le Pas, Manitoba (2008), Bishop Murray Chatlain of Mackenzie-Fort Smith, Northwest Territories (2009), the Catholic Bishops of Saskatchewan (2012), the Catholic Bishops of British Columbia and Yukon (2013), the Catholic Bishops of Alberta and the Northwest Territories (2014), Archbishop Terrence Prendergast of Ottawa, Ontario (2015), and Archbishop J. Michael Millar of Vancouver, British Columbia (2015).[14]

As an entity, the Canadian Conference of Catholic Bishops (CCCB) has issued numerous statements over the years: a *Statement by the National Meeting on Indian Residential Schools* (1991),[15] *Let Justice Flow Like a Mighty River: Brief by the Canadian Conference of Catholic Bishops to the Royal Commission on Aboriginal Peoples* (1995),[16] and "Launching of Truth and Reconciliation Commission: An Opportunity for Healing and Hope" (2008),[17] although the CCCB did not formally participate in the TRC process. Yet the various Catholic entities named in the *Indian Residential Schools Settlement Agreement* (2006) regarding compensation stemming from their participation in the Indian residential school system failed to meet their financial obligations set out therein[18] and were ultimately discharged of their financial obligations on 30 October 2015 due to their Best-Efforts Campaign falling well short of the $25 million goal. Although the CCCB itself is not included among the Catholic entities, upward of fifteen individual Roman Catholic archdioceses across Canada are named.[19] Given this reality, it is perhaps understandable that circumstances preceding what Pope Francis called his "penitential pilgrimage"[20] were not sufficient to credibly launch the reconciliatory process between the church and Indigenous peoples in Canada.

PAPAL APOLOGY: THE VATICAN, APRIL 2022

Given the history of the Catholic response to the *Settlement Agreement*, it is not surprising that the collective hierarchy of the Catholic Church in Canada has generally responded cautiously to truth and reconciliation. Many faithful Catholics believe in, support, and are working toward righting the church's relationship with all Indigenous peoples in Canada. But there can be no reconciliation without repentance. That it took the Canadian Conference of Catholic Bishops so long to reiterate its apology following the detection of unmarked graves at Indian residential schools in the spring and summer of 2021 was perhaps a sign of its own internal ambivalence about the role of the church in the residential school system.[21] Relying on distinctions of the structure of the Catholic Church in general to evade a renewed apology (e.g., there is no such entity as the Canadian Catholic Church),[22] the CCCB did not attend to the pastoral necessity of reiterating, as often and as deeply as necessary, its sorrow, apology, and repentance for the church's participation in what the TRC called a "cultural genocide"[23] and therefore failed Indigenous Peoples and Catholics across the land. After several months, its long-delayed apology came on 24 September 2021, followed by a pledge of $30 million on 27 September 2021.[24] These gestures appeared to set the stage for a series of papal apologies. The historical resistance of the CCCB to inviting Pope Francis to Canada

– a typical protocol for the pope to enter the pastoral jurisdiction of Canada's bishops – due both to the expense that would be incurred and to internal disagreement about how best to respond to Indigenous Peoples in Canada, along with Pope Francis's subsequent inability to offer an apology in 2018,[25] seemed a turning point for many Canadian Catholics. In the form of petitions, many concerned Catholics voiced their desire for the Canadian Conference of Catholic Bishops to undertake an apology and to initiate a papal visit to fulfill the TRC's call for a church apology months before the bishops did. The frustration among Canadian Catholics was palpable.[26]

Following its apology and financial pledge, the CCCB cooperated with First Nations, Inuit, and Métis groups across Canada to accompany a delegation to Rome in order to meet with Pope Francis. Following delays related to the Covid-19 pandemic, the meeting finally took place in the spring of 2022. [27] Between 28 and 31 March 2022, each of the First Nations, Métis, and Inuit delegations met privately with Pope Francis to offer accounts of their own and their ancestors' experiences in Indian Residential Schools in Canada. They recounted the unconscionable abuses perpetrated against them by Roman Catholic operators of the schools. They spoke of the tragic legacy of the schools for Indigenous people in Canada. They identified the current intergenerational trauma affecting Indigenous groups across Turtle Island. And they described the enduring resilience and strength of First Nations, Inuit, and Métis people. Pope Francis listened.

On 1 April 2022, Pope Francis responded to the delegates of Indigenous Peoples visiting him in Rome.[28] He recounted their stories to him, he apologized for the Catholic Church's role in operating Canadian Indian residential schools, and he promised to continue to journey with them toward reconciliation on their native lands in Canada. The fulfillment of this promise would be a concrete response to the TRC's call 58. The pope's initial apology to the Indigenous delegation was an opening gesture toward repentance and reconciliation.

PENITENTIAL PILGRIMAGE TO CANADA – CONTEXT

Pope Francis made good on his promise to visit Indigenous people on their native soil in July 2022. Over the course of six days, he met and spoke with Indigenous communities in numerous contexts in Alberta, Quebec, and Nunavut.[29] The pope's penitential pilgrimage was indeed historic. He met with Indigenous people in their sacred spaces and places of worship and spoke multiple times with large and small gatherings.[30]

Another of the TRC's *Calls to Action* was directly related to what is known as the Doctrine of Discovery: "We call upon federal, provincial, territorial, and municipal governments to repudiate concepts used to justify European sovereignty over Indigenous peoples and lands, such as the Doctrine of Discovery and *terra nullius,* and to reform those laws, government policies, and litigation strategies that continue to rely on such concepts."[31] Although this call is directed at various levels of government in Canada, the concepts within the Doctrine of Discovery are linked to numerous statements of the church and popes at the time of initial colonization (e.g., the bulls *Dum Diversas,* 1452; *Romanus Pontifex,* 1455; and *Inter Caetera,* 1493). Throughout Pope Francis's apostolic visit to Canada, there were calls among First Nations, Inuit, and Métis individuals and groups for him to repudiate the Doctrine of Discovery, which did not happen on Indigenous soil. However, on 30 March 2023, subsequent to Pope Francis's visit to Canada, the Vatican's press office issued a "Joint Statement of the Dicasteries for Culture and Education and for Promoting Integral Human Development on the 'Doctrine of Discovery." This document states, "In no uncertain terms, the Church's magisterium upholds the respect due to every human being. The Catholic Church therefore repudiates those concepts that fail to recognize the inherent human rights of indigenous peoples, including what has become known as the legal and political 'doctrine of discovery.'"[32] Included by some of this volume's authors are reflections on the Vatican's repudiation of the Doctrine of Discovery, as requested by the TRC in call 47.

OVERVIEW

This book seeks to represent perspectives on the papal visit both from those within the church and from those outside of it, including Indigenous studies scholars and theologians, Indigenous and non-Indigenous persons, individuals highly critical of the visit, and those who found the visit to be congenial, albeit at times unsatisfactory, to the work of reconciliation. Despite anticipating vociferous critique by some and general approval of the apologies by others, we were surprised by the confluence of perspectives from contributors with a very diverse range of backgrounds. For example, some of the harshest criticisms of the visit and its missed opportunities came from Catholic theologians, whereas some of the Indigenous writers – especially Niigaan Sinclair, co-author of the final chapter of this book with Darren Dias – were generally inclined to view the visit and the apologies as a step toward reconciliation. We believe that this confluence signals in itself a very positive development.

We have elected to organize this book outward from the Catholic worldview and theology, beginning with Donald Bolen, archbishop of Regina, whose work was pivotal to advocating for and organizing the papal visit to Canada. Bolen's chapter, "The Papal Apology and Seeds of an Action Plan," assesses the failures of the church candidly and recognizes the difficult road ahead given the general experience of distrust and pain. For Bolen, the work of faithful reconciliation begins with "building relationships with Indigenous communities" and "not only being ready to engage on all levels in solidarity with Indigenous communities as they strive to address inequalities, racism, and systemic injustices but also being ready to respond to those suffering the effects of intergenerational trauma." According to Bolen, the measure of the church's success is to be found in transformed relationships. Bolen references survivor Ted Quewezance of Keeseekoose First Nation in Saskatchewan, who "has frequently said that each survivor will need to make a decision about whether or not to accept the papal apology and that all survivors are on their own healing journey." Indeed, as Bolen argues, the seeds for an action plan were planted during this visit but will require careful tending, which involves faithful listening, the pursuit of justice, and support for the languages, cultures, and worldviews of Indigenous Peoples, including their knowledge and care for creation.

Christine Jamieson is an Indigenous Catholic theologian whose chapter, "Possibility and Impasse: The Authenticity of Pope Francis and the Messages Communicated by the Actions of the Catholic Church," assesses both the positive and the negative features of the papal visit based on her analysis of authenticity. Drawing on the philosophies of Emmanuel Levinas and Bernard Lonergan, Jamieson unpacks both the genuine encounters and the missed opportunities of the visit along the lines of what Levinas describes as the unconditional demand that the face of the other represents. As Jamieson puts it, "In its immediacy, the face of the other captures me and calls me to responsibility." Jamieson further develops the theme of responsibility to the other by understanding the pope's visit in terms of "incarnate meaning," arguing that both Indigenous survivors and Pope Francis were ultimately transformed by the encounter.

Annie Selak's chapter, "Bless You, Church, for You Have Sinned: An Ecclesiological Analysis of Papal Apologies and the Doctrine of Discovery," situates the papal apology within the context of other Catholic apologies, remarking on the similarities and differences between them. Among the important differences is this apology's grounding in past and future (or promised) actions. However, as Selak also notes, this apology falls short in its failure to acknowledge the church as the agent of the sinful acts for which Pope Francis apologizes. Selak also offers a textual analysis of this specific apology, as well as the subsequent repudiation of the Doctrine of Discovery. In both cases, the failure to decolonize the language of the church is palpable – in the former case because of the church's unwillingness to take full responsibility for its failures and in the latter case because of the sharp distinction that the church makes between itself and the Indigenous Peoples that it encountered during colonization and beyond.

Timothy Harvie writes as a settler Canadian who also belongs to the Roman Catholic tradition. His chapter, "Delocality and Colonial Apologies: A Critical Assessment of the Papal Apologies at Maskwacis and Lac

Ste Anne," is a critical analysis of Pope Francis's penitential pilgrimage in Alberta – both his apology at Maskwacis and the speech given at Lac Ste Anne. Harvie engages these texts in the light of Indigenous scholarship as well as the testimonies and conclusions of the Truth and Reconciliation Commission. Harvie argues that the pope's emphasis on the universal message of the gospel has the effect of delocalizing the actual communities that he is addressing, a move that is ultimately colonial in nature. As Harvie writes, "He decentred the particular in favour of the universal and displaced the land on which he stood in preference for biblical and metaphorical lands. The cumulative effect was a reinforcement of the hierarchical and colonial relationships that had been the cause of his pilgrimage in the first place." For Harvie, this universalization of Catholicism must be radically displaced in favour of local Indigenous communities and their wisdom.

Other voices speak in a similarly critical vein, although coming from a perspective outside of the Catholic Church. Chantal Fiola is a Manitoba Métis scholar whose work has been the patient recovery – through archival records and oral history – of traditional Métis spirituality, which had long been supressed by the church and by the Catholic Métis culture of the Prairies.[33] Her chapter, "The Papal Apology and Its Impacts on the Métis: Now What?" probes the effect of the papal visit on Métis communities. Given that the Métis today practise traditional Indigenous spirituality, Christianity, or a combination of the two, the papal visit was met with ambivalence by many members of Métis communities. Indeed, not only has ceremony always been practised by Métis communities, but it is also experiencing a resurgence. The papal visit had the effect of bringing some of the conflict between Catholics and traditional Métis into relief and even exposed Catholicism's institutional bias against traditional ceremony and its repression by the church. In this sense, the papal visit was a revisiting of painful memories of abuse, suppression, and the denial of the legitimacy of Indigenous ways of knowing.

The penultimate chapter of this book is written by an expert on ecclesial apologies, Jeremy M. Bergen. Bergen, a settler Mennonite theologian, takes a broad view of this apology from the perspective of regarding apologies as a political practice. In "The Political Practice of Canadian Church Apologies to Indigenous Peoples," Bergen examines the precisely political implications of ecclesial apologies. In this chapter, Bergen examines the recent papal apologies alongside apologies both by other Canadian churches and by Canadian Catholic organizations. Drawing on the work of Canadian philosopher Alice MacLachlan and Australian sociologist Danielle Celermajer, this chapter examines the practical possibilities of the pope's apology to Indian residential school survivors and its limitations.

This book concludes with a joint analysis by Niigaan Sinclair and Darren Dias titled "The Pilgrim Church in Canada: A Penitential People and the 2022 Papal Visit." In this chapter, the authors do not move from the particular (i.e., ecclesial) to the universal or political dimensions of the apology in the visit but instead offer a perspective of the visit as an expression of solidarity with the poor. For Sinclair and Dias, the penitential pilgrimage of the summer of 2022 may be understood in terms of "movement as performative action," one that invited Canadians more generally to travel from the centre to the periphery. Thus, according to Sinclair and Dias, this journey, although flawed, was a successful movement toward fulfilling the TRC's call 58, for it offered a clear path toward reconciliation – by beginning with penance. Therefore, this book, which is a largely critical investigation of the apology, has as its coda a chapter jointly written by an Indigenous and a Catholic scholar, which offers a constructive – and a hopeful – trajectory in which Pope Francis stands as an ambivalent, but nonetheless vital, ally to Indigenous Peoples globally.

As editors, we are inclined to echo this hopeful trajectory as we witness and affirm the unfolding and evolving nature of repentance, atonement, forgiveness, and reconciliation. For all of us woven within the history and aftermath of the Indian residential schools run by Catholic institutions on Turtle Island, this process is the work of lifetimes. Our hope is that the reflections offered here contribute meaningfully to the journey of reconciliation.

One suggestion about the reading of this volume may be helpful. This volume does not seek to harmonize the divergent responses of contributors into a cohesive narrative but instead invites readers to engage with a diversity of Indigenous and non-Indigenous voices, each grappling in its own way with the meanings, limitations, and possibilities of the pope's words and presence. By reading these contributions together, rather than in isolation, the reader may find that the broader historical, spiritual, and political implications of the visit are displayed in the collection. It is our hope that such a representation of divergent perspectives resists easy conclusions and honours the ongoing nature of truth, atonement, healing, and reconciliation.

NOTES

1 Eve Tuck and K. Wayne Yang, "Decolonization Is Not a Metaphor," *Decolonization: Indigeneity, Education, and Society* 1, no. 1 (2012): 1.

2 Office of the Chief, Tk'emlúps te Secwépemc (Kamloops Indian Band), "Statement from Tk'emlúps te Secwépemc Chief and Council Regarding Cowessess First Nation Unmarked Grave Findings," 24 June 2021, https://tkemlups.ca/news/statement-from-tkemlups-te-secwepemc-chief-and-council-regarding-cowessess-first-nation-unmarked-grave-findings/.

3 Oblates of Mary Immaculate, Lacombe, Canada, "Schools Where Oblates Worked," n.d., omilacombe.ca/helpful-documents-and-resources/.

4 Truth and Reconciliation Commission of Canada (TRC), *Calls to Action* (2015), nos 71–6, https://www2.gov.bc.ca/assets/gov/british-columbians-our-governments/indigenous-people/aboriginal-peoples-documents/calls_to_action_english2.pdf. The Truth and Reconciliation Commission of Canada undertook a six-year process of listening to, acknowledging, honouring, and recording the stories of survivors of the Indian residential schools and their families. The TRC travelled across the country to hear from witnesses, engage and educate the public, and chart a historical record of the residential school system in Canada. In 2015, at the close of its work, the TRC issued a multi-volume report, which included ninety-four recommendations published under the title *Calls to Action*. The records and legacies of the TRC are now housed with the National Centre for

Truth and Reconciliation, which continues the work of the TRC (see https://nctr.ca).

5 Canadian Press, "Timeline of Events since Finding of Unmarked Graves in Kamloops," *CTV News*, 18 May 2022, http://www.ctvnews.ca/canada/timeline-of-events-since-finding-of-unmarked-graves-in-kamloops-1.5908292. For an updated list of residential schools at which unmarked graves have been located, see "Table: Residential Schools That Have Discovered Unmarked Graves," *Indigenous Watchdog*, 30 July 2023, https://www.indigenouswatchdog.org/update/residential-schools-that-have-discovered-unmarked-graves/.

6 On 31 May 2024, the original two-year term of the special interlocutor was extended to the fall of 2024. Office of the Independent Special Interlocutor, "News Release," 31 May 2024, https://osi-bis.ca/wp-content/uploads/2024/05/NR-Work-of-Special-Interlocutor-May-Update-FINAL-EN.pdf.

7 Office of the Independent Special Interlocutor, "Mandate," n.d., https://osi-bis.ca/about#mandate.

8 Independent Special Interlocutor, *Sacred Responsibility: Searching for the Missing Children and Unmarked Burials – Interim Report* (2023), https://osi-bis.ca/wp-content/uploads/2023/06/OSI_InterimReport_June-2023_WEB.pdf; Independent Special Interlocutor, *Sites of Truth, Sites of Conscience: Unmarked Burials and Mass Graves of Missing and Disappeared Indigenous Children in Canada* (2024), https://osi-bis.ca/historical-report/.

9 Office of the Independent Special Interlocutor, n.d., https://osi-bis.ca.

10 TRC, *Calls to Action*, no. 58.

11 Vatican, "Canada: Communiqué of the Holy See Press Office," 29 April 2009, https://www.vatican.va/resources/resources_canada-first-nations-apr2009_en.html; "Phil Fontaine's Statement to the Pope on Residential Schools Apology," *Georgia Straight*, 29 April 2009, https://www.straight.com/blogra/phil-fontaines-statement-pope-residential-schools-apology.

12 Elizabeth McSheffrey, "Something Is Different about This Trip to the Vatican: Phil Fontaine Says It's 'Hope,'" *Global News*, 30 March 2022, https://globalnews.ca/news/8721907/phil-fontaine-hope-second-vatican-delegation/.

13 Oblate Conference of Canada, "An Apology to the First Nations of Canada by the Oblate Conference of Canada," 24 July 1991, https://omila combe.ca/wp-content/uploads/2021/06/AN-APOLOGY-TO-THE-FIRST-NATIONS-OF-CANADA-BY-THE-OBLATE-CONFER ENCE-OF-CANADA-w-intro-1991.pdf; Canadian Religious Conference, "Statement on Behalf of Congregations of Women Religious Involved in the Indian Residential Schools of Canada," 16 January 2014, https://crc-canada.org/en/statement-congregations-women-religious-involved-indian-residential-schools-canada/. First issued in April 2009 in Rome, this statement was adapted for presentation to the TRC in September 2013 in Vancouver.

14 With the exception of the statements of Bishop Albert LeGatt of Saskatoon and Archbishop Sylvain Lavoie of Keewatin–Le Pas, which were verbal apologies made on 9 March 2008 at the Remembering the Children event, links to these apologies are available on the CCCB website at https://www.cccb.ca/indigenous-peoples/chronology-of-cccb-engage ment/. The Roman Catholic Diocese of Saskatoon has listed the verbal apologies of LeGatt and Lavoie at https://rcdos.ca/wp-content/uploads/2021/06/catholic_apologies_list_2.pdf.

15 Canadian Conference of Catholic Bishops, *Statement by the National Meeting on Indian Residential Schools* (1991), https://www.cccb.ca/wp-content/uploads/2017/10/apology_saskatoon.pdf.

16 Canadian Conference of Catholic Bishops, *Let Justice Flow Like a Mighty River: Brief by the Canadian Conference of Catholic Bishops to the Royal Commission on Aboriginal Peoples* (1995), https://www.cccb.ca/wp-content/uploads/2017/10/let_justice_flow_like_a_mighty_river.pdf.

17 Canadian Conference of Catholic Bishops, "Launching of Truth and Reconciliation Commission: An Opportunity for Healing and Hope," 1 May 2008, https://www.cccb.ca/media-release/launching-of-truth-and-reconciliation-commission-an-opportunity-for-healing-and-hope/.

18 Government of Canada, *Indian Residential Schools Settlement Agreement: Schedule O-3, Catholic Entities* (2006), https://www.residentialschoolsettle ment.ca/Schedule_O-3.pdf. See also Canadian Conference of Catholic Bishops, "Canada's Bishops Provide Update on Indian Residential Schools

Settlement Agreement," 28 January 2022, https://www.cccb.ca/indigenous-peoples/indian-residential-schools-and-trc/canadas-bishops-provide-up date-on-indian-residential-school-settlement-agreement/.

19 Government of Canada, *Indian Residential Schools Settlement Agreement: Schedule C, Corporate Catholic Defendants* (2006), https://www.residential schoolsettlement.ca/Schedule_C.PDF.

20 Pope Francis, "Angelus," 17 July 2022, https://www.vatican.va/content/francesco/en/angelus/2022/documents/20220717-angelus.html.

21 Deborah Gyapong, "Bishops Not Ready to Invite Pope Francis to Canada," *Catholic Register*, 1 October 2017, 3, https://archive.catholicregister.org/library//The_Catholic_Register_10_01_2017.pdf#page=3&viewrect=0,610,500,500&highlight=40,218,197,188; Michael Swan, "Canada Is Not in Pope's Travel Plans," *Catholic Register*, 1 April 2018, 3, https://archive.catholicregister.org/library//The_Catholic_Register_04_01_2018.pdf#page=3&viewrect=0,0,500,500&highlight=40,176,830,815.

22 Archdiocese of Toronto, "Frequently Asked Questions Regarding Residential Schools," June 2021, https://www.archtoronto.org/siteassets/media/archdiocese-of-toronto-main-site/files/press-releases/2021/residen tial-schools—-frequently-asked-questions—-june-2021.pdf.

23 Truth and Reconciliation Commission of Canada, *Honouring the Truth, Reconciling for the Future: Summary of the Final Report of the Truth and Reconciliation Commission of Canada* (2015), 1, https://ehprnh2mwo3.exact dn.com/wp-content/uploads/2021/01/Executive_Summary_English_Web.pdf.

24 Canadian Conference of Catholic Bishops, "Statement of Apology by the Catholic Bishops of Canada to the Indigenous Peoples of This Land," 24 September 2021, https://www.cccb.ca/wp-content/uploads/2021/09/Statement_from_CBC_to_Indigenous-EN.pdf; Canadian Conference of Catholic Bishops, "Canadian Bishops Announce $30M National Financial Pledge to Support Healing and Reconciliation Initiatives," 27 September 2021, https://www.cccb.ca/media-release/canadian-bishops-announce-30m-national-financial-pledge-to-support-healing-and-reconciliation-initiatives/.

25 Jorge Barrera, "Lack of Bishops' Consensus, Concerns over Cost behind Pope Apology Decision: Archbishop," CBC *News*, 26 April 2018, https://www.cbc.ca/news/indigenous/cost-lack-of-consensus-behind-pope-apology-decision-1.4635802; Jason Warick, "Renewed Calls for Pope to Visit Sask. to Apologize for Residential Schools after 2017 Effort Failed," CBC *News*, 8 June 2021, https://www.cbc.ca/news/canada/saskatoon/saskatchewan-chief-residential-schools-pope-francis-1.6057016; Dean Dettloff, "Why Hasn't Pope Francis Apologized in Canada? Ask the Bishops," *National Catholic Reporter*, 6 July 2021, https://www.ncronline.org/news/guest-voices/why-hasnt-pope-francis-apologized-canada-ask-bishops.

26 Sam Bianco, initiator, "Statement from Concerned Canadian Catholics on the Discoveries in Kamloops," *Change.org*, 4 June 2021, https://www.change.org/p/canadian-conference-of-catholic-bishops-statement-from-concerned-canadian-catholics-on-the-discoveries-in-kamloops-fdaf3705-463e-4bac-9354-b8203a4762a6; Hon. George Valin and Maurice Switzer, initiators, "Call for Papal Apology for Residential School Abuses," *Change.org*, 5 June 2021, https://www.change.org/p/call-for-papal-apology-for-residential-school-abuses. Together, these petitions garnered over 70,000 signatures.

27 Canadian Conference of Catholic Bishops, "Canadian Catholic Bishops, Assembly of First Nations, Métis National Council, and Inuit Tapiriit Kanatami Provide an Update on Delegation to Rome," 7 December 2021, https://www.cccb.ca/announcement/canadian-bishops-assembly-of-first-nations-metis-national-council-and-inuit-tapiriit-kanatami-provide-an-update-on-delegation-to-rome/; Canadian Conference of Catholic Bishops, "Canadian Bishops and Indigenous Delegates Depart on Historic Trip to the Holy See," 24 March 2022, https://www.cccb.ca/media-release/canadian-bishops-and-indigenous-delegates-depart-on-historic-trip-to-the-holy-see/.

28 Pope Francis, "Address of His Holiness Pope Francis: Clementine Hall," 1 April 2022, https://www.vatican.va/content/francesco/en/speeches/2022/april/documents/20220401-popoli-indigeni-canada.html.

29 Canadian Conference of Catholic Bishops, "Pope Francis' Penitential Pilgrimage," n.d., https://www.cccb.ca/indigenous-peoples/pope-francis-penitential-pilgrimage/.

30 For a listing of and access to all of Pope Francis's addresses during his penitential pilgrimage, see Vatican, "Apostolic Journey of His Holiness Pope Francis to Canada, 24–30 July 2022," 23 June 2022, https://www.vatican.va/content/francesco/en/travels/2022/outside/documents/canada-2022.html.

31 TRC, *Calls to Action*, no. 47.

32 Holy See Press Office, "Joint Statement of the Dicasteries for Culture and Education and for Promoting Integral Human Development on the 'Doctrine of Discovery,'" 30 March 2023, para. 7, https://press.vatican.va/content/salastampa/it/bollettino/pubblico/2023/03/30/0238/00515.html.

33 Chantal Fiola, *Rekindling the Sacred Fire: Métis Ancestry and Anishinaabe Spirituality* (Winnipeg: University of Manitoba Press, 2015); Chantal Fiola, *Returning to Ceremony: Spirituality in Manitoba Métis Communities* (Winnipeg: University of Manitoba Press, 2021).

I

The Papal Apology and Seeds of an Action Plan

Donald Bolen

In the lead-up to both the visit of Indigenous delegations to Rome from 28 March to 1 April 2022 and the visit of Pope Francis to Canada in July of that year, there was much conversation about the shape and content of the apology that Pope Francis should offer to the Indigenous Peoples of Canada. As one of those involved in the preparation of these encounters and in dialogues on local and national levels with survivors of residential schools, I was able to hear many hopes and expectations connected with a response to the Truth and Reconciliation Commission of Canada's advocacy of a papal apology in call 58 of its *Calls to Action* (2015).[1]

There was a wide range of perspectives in Indigenous communities about what would be most helpful for the pope to say, but some of the central elements expected of an apology were the following:

- that it would acknowledge all that Indigenous people suffered at residential schools, including that Indigenous children were taken from their homes and separated from their parents and grandparents; that Indigenous languages were suppressed and that cultural and spiritual traditions were denigrated; that many children suffered physical, sexual, psychological, emotional, and spiritual abuses; and that many children died while at residential schools;

- that it would take responsibility on behalf of the Catholic Church for the suffering that was experienced at Catholic-operated residential schools and that remains a legacy of these schools;
- that it would acknowledge the trauma of survivors and the intergenerational trauma experienced by many First Nations, Métis, and Inuit communities;
- that it would express real lament and sorrow as well as a commitment to make changes in light of what has been learned through the truth and reconciliation process;
- that it would be offered at the site of a former residential school, preferably one where ground penetrating radar had identified possible unmarked graves, and that the many specific requests for the pope to visit particular places (e.g., residential schools in the province of Saskatchewan in the cities of Kamloops and Winnipeg), each extended with hopes and expectations, would be honoured;
- that it would be connected to reparation, financial support, and other means of responding to the waves of suffering that are the legacy of residential schools;
- that it would be followed by an action plan agreed to by Canadian bishops, preferably one embedded in the papal visit itself, that would move the church toward real conciliation through practical steps of solidarity – an expectation that invited a focus, even in the planning of the visit, on the importance of "the day after the apology";[2]
- that it would address how the schools were an extension of a colonization that had led to the taking of Indigenous lands and to the marginalizing of Indigenous Peoples and that the pope would repudiate the papal bulls that had provided support to the colonizers' understanding that they were discovering lands that could then be claimed and occupied, with no regard for the fact that the lands had been inhabited by Indigenous Peoples for thousands of years.

There was a recognition that all survivors would need to make their own decision about how to respond to whatever apology was given.

As the papal visit unfolded over the course of six days in late July 2022,[3] the events and addresses were carefully scrutinized, with media outlets presenting a wide range of feedback. Although a varied response was to be expected, the visit was planned as a whole. It is therefore both helpful and appropriate to work with the corpus of Pope Francis's presented texts as a single unit, taking into account that they were accompanied by his actions and gestures over the course of the visit, in analyzing the content of the apology that was given and the way forward that was to some degree charted out.

This chapter does not offer an extensive evaluation of the papal apology but aims to extract and synthesize the substance of what was said. The first section identifies elements of the apology extended by Pope Francis, and the second section looks at traces of an action plan that were identified and expanded upon as a follow-up to the apology. A brief third section addresses the statement on the Doctrine of Discovery presented by the Holy See, which was published on 30 March 2023, eight months after the papal visit.

COMPONENTS OF THE PAPAL APOLOGY

In this section, I lay out six key components of the papal apology: it addressed the reality that many children died in residential schools; it acknowledged the suffering of Indigenous people attending the schools; it was extended on behalf of the church; it acknowledged the residential school system's part in a colonizing effort to assimilate Indigenous Peoples, a system devastating for them; it acknowledged the trauma and intergenerational trauma that Indigenous survivors, their families, and their communities continue to carry; and it interpreted the wounds inflicted by the school system from a theological perspective, regarding them as instances of Christ crucified in those who suffered in residential schools.

Acknowledging the Children Who Never Came Home

In the days leading up to the papal visit, Pope Francis called his trip to Canada a "penitential pilgrimage," adding that it was different from other papal trips that he had taken.[4] Although it was not identified as an apology tour, significant words of apology were extended at each location of the visit, and they were very much at the heart of the visit.

The first public event of the papal visit was held at the site of the former Ermineskin Indian Residential School at Maskwacis, south of Edmonton. Upon arrival at the site, Pope Francis prayed at the cemetery, where it is understood that there are remains of children who died while attending the school. He then entered the church on the site, where the National Centre for Truth and Reconciliation had unfurled the banner of the names on the "Student Memorial Register," remembering the children who never returned home from residential schools. There, the pope prayed before the list of names, and he blessed and kissed the banner.

At the start of his address, the pope made reference to the two pairs of children's moccasins that had been presented to him by retired chief Mary Ann Daywalker-Pelletier of Okanese First Nation during the meeting of the First Nation delegation with Pope Francis in Rome on 31 March 2022. The moccasins were presented as a living reminder of the children who died while at residential school, with the request that the pope return the moccasins when he came to Canada with an apology.

Acknowledgment of All That Was Suffered in Residential Schools

In his address to the Maskwacis First Nation, Pope Francis acknowledged what he had heard from the Indigenous delegations months earlier:

> Again, I think back on the stories you told: how the policies of assimilation ended up systematically marginalizing the indigenous peoples; how also through the system of residential schools your languages and cultures were denigrated and suppressed; how children suffered physical, verbal, psychological and spiritual abuse; how they

> were taken away from their homes at a young age, and how that indelibly affected relationships between parents and children, grandparents and grandchildren.

The apology that followed built on this acknowledgment of both the suffering that Indigenous people experienced in residential schools and how assimilation policies, including the residential school system, "were devastating for the people of these lands."

> I am here because the first step of my penitential pilgrimage among you is that of again asking forgiveness, of telling you once more that I am deeply sorry. Sorry for the ways in which, regrettably, many Christians supported the colonizing mentality of the powers that oppressed the indigenous peoples. I am sorry. I ask forgiveness, in particular, for the ways in which many members of the Church and of religious communities cooperated, not least through their indifference, in projects of cultural destruction and forced assimilation promoted by the governments of that time, which culminated in the system of residential schools.[5]

Three days later, at the Cathedral-Basilica of Notre-Dame de Québec, he also addressed the legacy of sexual abuse of minors and vulnerable people in contexts that included but were not limited to residential schools. Pope Francis noted that this scandal required "firm action and an irreversible commitment. Together with you, I would like once more to ask forgiveness of all the victims. The pain and the shame we feel must become an occasion for conversion: never again!"[6]

An Apology on Behalf of the Church

One question raised in Indigenous communities and highlighted in the media, both after Pope Francis's apology in Rome on 1 April 2022 and during his visit to Canada, was whether his apology acknowledged only the sinful behaviour of a few individuals or acknowledged the Catholic

Church's responsibility and apologized on behalf of the church as an institution. At Maskwacis, he introduced a distinction that is relevant here by noting – in the same sentence – that "although … there were many outstanding instances of devotion and care for children, the overall effects of the policies linked to the residential schools were catastrophic." He then proceeded to offer a strong critique of the church's engagement with the system itself:

> What our Christian faith tells us is that this was a disastrous error, incompatible with the Gospel of Jesus Christ. It is painful to think of how the firm soil of values, language and culture that made up the authentic identity of your peoples was eroded, and that you have continued to pay the price of this.

When the pope proceeded to speak of "many Christians" who were responsible for the evil committed against Indigenous Peoples[7] – a phrase that he echoed at Sacred Heart Church of the First Peoples in Edmonton and at the Citadelle de Québec – he made clear that he was speaking not only of those who had abused Indigenous children but also of those who had supported or been indifferent to the church's engagement in the system itself. At Sacred Heart Church, he noted,

> It pains me to think that Catholics contributed to policies of assimilation and enfranchisement that inculcated a sense of inferiority, robbing communities and individuals of their cultural and spiritual identity, severing their roots and fostering prejudicial and discriminatory attitudes; and that this was also done in the name of an educational system that was supposedly Christian.[8]

One further point in this regard emerged during a question-and-answer session in Quebec City with members of the Jesuit community in Canada, where the pope was queried about how they should respond when asked why the pope was apologizing on behalf of Christians but not on behalf of the Church as an institution. He responded by noting that by virtue of his role as pope, he always speaks "in the name of the Church, not in my own name. I speak in the name of the Church even when I do not make it explicit," the exception being when he explicitly notes that he is sharing a personal thought and not speaking in the name of the church.[9]

Cooperation with Colonizing Attitudes and a System of Assimilation

In the apology offered at the Citadelle de Québec, the focus was increasingly placed on the acceptance within the Christian community of governmental policies of assimilation and a colonizing mentality. "In that deplorable system, promoted by the governmental authorities of the time, which separated many children from their families, different local Catholic institutions had a part." He acknowledged that "'the history of suffering'" within Indigenous communities – what he called "the fruit of the colonizing mentality" – "'does not heal easily.'"[10]

In Iqaluit, too, the apology was contextualized in terms of engagement with a residential school system grounded in "policies of cultural assimilation and enfranchisement." There, the pope noted "how evil it is to break the bonds uniting parents and children, to damage our closest relationships," and he relayed the testimony of an elder who had contrasted the spirit within Indigenous families before and after their experience of the residential school system:

> [The elder] compared those days, when grandparents, parents and children were harmoniously together, to springtime, when young birds chirp happily around their mother. But suddenly – he said – the singing stopped: families were broken up, and the little ones were taken away far from home. Winter fell over everything.[11]

Although Pope Francis did not directly address the papal bulls of the fifteenth century, which were often associated with the Doctrine of Discovery during the visit, he communicated a strong critique of colonization and of cooperation within the Christian community with policies of assimilation. At the Cathedral-Basilica of Notre-Dame de Québec, he stated strongly, "Never again can the Christian community allow itself to be infected by the idea that one culture is superior to others, or that it is legitimate to employ ways of coercing others."[12] It was communicated during the course of the papal visit that the Holy See would be issuing a further statement on the Doctrine of Discovery in due course. And during the press conference on the flight back to Rome, he spoke of the genocidal character of taking children from their families and suppressing culture, traditions, and worldview.

Acknowledgment of Trauma and Intergenerational Trauma

At his address to the Indigenous delegations in Rome, Pope Francis not only detailed what he had heard from those he had met with but also referred to the "unresolved traumas that have become intergenerational traumas."[13] At the outset of his visit to Canada, at Maskwacis, he acknowledged that even his presence here on Canadian soil would evoke trauma for some by surfacing memories of devastating experiences in residential schools:

> These are traumas that are in some way reawakened whenever the subject comes up; I realize too that our meeting today can bring back old memories and hurts, and that many of you may feel uncomfortable even as I speak.[14]

He thanked survivors for telling him "about the heavy burdens that you still bear, for sharing with me these bitter memories," noting that even though costly, "it is right to remember, because forgetfulness leads to indifference."[15]

Pope Francis proceeded to recognize that although he was not able to visit many of the places to which he had been invited, he was "aware of the sufferings and traumas, the difficulties and challenges, experienced by the indigenous peoples in every region of this country." In the journey forward, he stressed that it would be important "to assist the survivors of the residential schools to experience healing from the traumas they suffered."[16] And at Lac Ste Anne, he made reference to "traumatic experiences that no human consolation can ever heal."[17]

Although he did not use the language of intergenerational trauma during the course of his visit to Canada, he pointed to its reality, to "the scars of still open wounds,"[18] and to ongoing suffering within Indigenous communities.

A Christian Interpretation of Indigenous Suffering

Although it was clear that Pope Francis was mindful of speaking both to Indigenous and to non-Indigenous people and both to Catholics and to people with a wide spectrum of worldviews and faith traditions, his apology did grow out of a very particular article of faith. This matter was most clearly expressed at Sacred Heart Church in Edmonton, where the pope spoke to a church gathering about two approaches to evangelization with very different ways of exercising power and authority. He pointed to the lasting pain created when Christians and ecclesial institutions "imposed their own cultural models" and "forced God" on students, noting that this conduct was not God's way. By contrast, God loves us, liberates us, and leaves us free.

> One cannot proclaim God in a way contrary to God himself. And yet, how many times has this happened in history! While God presents himself simply and quietly, we always have the temptation to impose him, and to impose ourselves in his name. It is the worldly temptation to make him come down from the cross and show himself with power … Brothers and sisters, in the name of Jesus, may this never happen again in the Church. May Jesus be preached as he desires, in freedom and charity. In every crucified person whom we meet, may we see not a problem to be solved, but a brother or sister to be loved, the flesh of Christ to be loved.[19]

In this context, Pope Francis spoke of "Christ, crucified in the many students of the residential schools."[20] This interpretation of Indigenous suffering provides a very different lens through which to view the presence of God in the context of residential schools: God is in and with the little ones and in their suffering. Although there was no request to survivors that they view or receive the pope's apology through the lens of his faith perspective, this theological framework informed the apology that was offered.

ELEMENTS OF AN ACTION PLAN EMERGING FROM THE APOLOGY

In the Truth and Reconciliation Commission's *Final Report* (2015), the commentary on call 58 notes, "Apologies mark only a beginning point on pathways of reconciliation; the proof of their authenticity lies in putting words into action."[21]

Meeting with the Indigenous delegations in Rome, Pope Francis had noted that "any truly effective process of healing requires concrete actions."[22] At the start of his visit to Canada, Pope Francis expressed his agreement with the Truth and Reconciliation Commission's request for engagement following an apology:

> Dear brothers and sisters, many of you and your representatives have stated that begging pardon is not the end of the matter. I fully agree: that is only the first step, the starting point. I also recognize that, "looking to the past, no effort to beg pardon and to seek to repair the harm done will ever be sufficient" and that, "looking ahead to the future, no effort must be spared to create a culture able to prevent such situations from happening."[23]

Although Pope Francis did not explicitly lay out an action plan for the Catholic Church in Canada, he did empower it to engage with Indigenous communities on a path toward healing, reconciliation, and solidarity. In various ways, he pointed to the importance of building relationships between Indigenous and non-Indigenous people, relationships shaped both by attentiveness to the needs of the other and by a desire to walk together. At Sacred Heart Church, he stressed that this engagement needed to happen at the local level:

> Dear brothers and sisters: gestures and visits can be important, but most words and deeds of reconciliation take place at the local level, in communities like this, where individuals and families travel side-by-side, day by day. To pray together, to help one another, to share life stories, common joys and common struggles: this is what opens the door to the reconciling work of God.[24]

He also gave indicators of what the path forward would require on both the local and the national levels. In this section of the chapter, I highlight four areas where Pope Francis summoned the church to engagement: telling the truth about the past; standing in solidarity with Indigenous Peoples in their rightful pursuit of justice; offering support for the recovery and strengthening of Indigenous languages and cultures; and emphasizing the beauty and importance of an Indigenous understanding of creation and of relations with the land and environment.

Commitment to the Transparent Search for Truth

At his meeting with Indigenous delegations in Rome, Pope Francis noted,

> Without historical memory and without a commitment to learning from past mistakes, problems remain unresolved and keep coming back … The memory of the past must never be sacrificed at the altar of alleged progress … In a fraternal spirit, I encourage the Bishops and the Catholic community to continue taking steps towards the transparent search for truth and to foster healing and reconciliation.[25]

It is telling that Pope Francis began his trip to Canada in Maskwacis by focusing on an honest attentiveness to the past and by calling not only for a deeper investigation "into the facts of what took place" but also for the creation of "space for memory." He added, "Here, today, I am with you to recall the past, to grieve with you, to bow our heads together in silence and to pray before the graves."[26]

Meeting with an Indigenous delegation in Quebec City, he framed the purpose of his visit in relation to the critical role of truth telling in the move toward a future of right relationships:

> I have come … so that progress may be made in the search for truth, so that the processes of healing and reconciliation may continue, and so that seeds of hope can keep being sown for future generations – indigenous and non-indigenous alike – who desire to live together, in harmony, as brothers and sisters.[27]

For the church in Canada, following this path will entail, among other things, ongoing research on the historical experience of Indigenous Peoples at the time of colonization and of residential schools; assistance to First Nations, Métis, and Inuit communities where there was a Catholic-operated residential school as the church engages in archival work to better understand what happened there; and working with Catholic schools and ongoing adult education systems in the preparation of curriculum and programs that provide an accurate account of the residential school legacy, of treaties, and of intergenerational trauma.

Commitment to Walking with Indigenous Peoples in Pursuit of Justice

Survivors of residential schools have repeatedly asked churches and society as a whole to support the inherent rights of Indigenous Peoples, rights given them by the Creator and articulated in the United Nations Declaration on the Rights of Indigenous Peoples (2007).[28]

It was at the Citadelle de Québec that Pope Francis spoke most directly to the injustice and inequality experienced by Indigenous Peoples in Canada and to the importance of making economic and social decisions that addressed their needs. This challenge was extended both to the church and to society as a whole:

> Even in a country as developed and prosperous as Canada, which pays great attention to social assistance, there are many homeless persons who turn to churches and food banks to receive essential help in meeting their needs, which, lest we forget, are not only material. These brothers and sisters of ours spur us to reflect on the urgent need for efforts to remedy the radical injustice that taints our world, in which the abundance of the gifts of creation is unequally distributed. It is scandalous that the well-being generated by economic development does not benefit all the sectors of society. And it is indeed sad that precisely among the native peoples we often find many indices of poverty, along with other negative indicators, such as the low percentage of schooling, and less than easy access to owning a home and to health care.[29]

The pope proceeded to point to the Truth and Reconciliation Commission's *Calls to Action* (2015) and to the United Nations Declaration on the Rights of Indigenous Peoples (2007) as guideposts for moving toward a more just society.[30]

At Commonwealth Stadium in Edmonton, he offered a vision of what a future where justice flourished might look like:

> A future in which the elderly are not cast aside because, from a "practical" standpoint, they are "no longer useful." A future that does not judge the value of people simply by what they can produce. A future that is not indifferent to the need of the aged to be cared for and listened to. A future in which the history of violence and marginalization suffered by our indigenous brothers and sisters

> is never repeated … Let us move forward together, and together, let us dream.[31]

For the Catholic Church in Canada, being an ally in the rightful pursuit of justice will require building relationships with Indigenous communities, listening to the needs of survivors, and not only being ready to engage on all levels in solidarity with Indigenous communities as they strive to address inequalities, racism, and systemic injustices but also being ready to respond to those suffering the effects of intergenerational trauma.

Support of Indigenous Languages, Cultures, and Worldview

As noted above, during the course of his visit to Canada, Pope Francis expressed how wrong it was that Indigenous languages and cultures had been suppressed, and he acknowledged the devastating impact of this loss. But he also highlighted his great respect for Indigenous languages and cultures at each location that he visited. At Maskwacis, speaking of traditions passed on for thousands of years, he noted,

> You learned to foster a sense of family and community, and to build solid bonds between generations, honouring your elders and caring for your little ones. A treasury of sound customs and teachings, centred on concern for others, truthfulness, courage and respect, humility, honesty and practical wisdom![32]

At Lac Ste Anne, on the occasion of the feast of Saints Anne and Joachim, grandparents of Jesus, he celebrated the presence and blessings of Indigenous grandmothers and noted, "I am struck by the vital role of women in indigenous communities: they occupy a prominent place as blessed sources not only of physical but also of spiritual life."[33]

At the Citadelle de Québec, he spoke of how Indigenous culture "is of great help in recalling the importance of social values" and commented,

> The indigenous peoples have much to teach us about care and protection for the family; among them, from an early age, children learn

> to recognize right from wrong, to be truthful, to share, to correct mistakes, to begin anew, to comfort one another and to be reconciled.[34]

In Iqaluit, he reflected on how Inuit peoples have passed on from generation to generation "such basic values as respect for the elderly, genuine fraternity and care for the environment." He specifically encouraged the young people to listen to the wisdom of their elders and to celebrate their culture and their "beautiful Inuktitut language."[35]

When Pope Francis returned to Rome, at his weekly public audience, he spoke of his visit to Canada, noting how he had "reaffirmed the active will of the Holy See and the local Catholic communities to promote the Indigenous cultures, with appropriate spiritual paths and with attention to the customs and languages of the peoples," and he spoke of the need to "recover harmony between modernity and ancestral cultures."[36] His visit to Canada encouraged a deep engagement with Indigenous Peoples on the level of culture and worldviews. In Maskwacis, Pope Francis commented, "When the European colonists first arrived here, there was a great opportunity to bring about a fruitful encounter between cultures, traditions and forms of spirituality. Yet for the most part that did not happen."[37] Although the suppression of Indigenous ways in the past is to be acknowledged and mourned, the possibility still exists today for the Christian communities to support the recovery and strengthening of Indigenous languages, traditions, and cultures while being receptive to the possibility of encountering the riches of those ways.

The Blessing of the Indigenous Understanding of Creation and the Land

Throughout his pontificate, Pope Francis paid significant attention to the environment and to care for the earth, and in the most important documents to treat this subject, he highlighted the wisdom of Indigenous Peoples with regard to creation. In his encyclical on the environment, *Laudato Si'* (2015), Pope Francis noted that in caring for creation,

> It is essential to show special care for indigenous communities and their cultural traditions. They are not merely one minority among others, but should be the principal dialogue partners, especially when large projects affecting their land are proposed. For them, land is not a commodity but rather a gift from God and from their ancestors who rest there, a sacred space with which they need to interact if they are to maintain their identity and values. When they remain on their land, they themselves care for it best.[38]

In the apostolic exhortation that followed the Synod on the Amazon, held in Rome in October 2019, he spoke of how the Indigenous Peoples of the Amazon "care for ecosystems and they recognize that the earth, while serving as a generous source of support for their life, also has a maternal dimension that evokes respect and tender love."[39]

It was not surprising, then, that Pope Francis would speak of Indigenous respect for the land and creation when visiting the Indigenous Peoples of Canada. At Maskwacis, he noted,

> Brothers and sisters, you have lived on these lands for thousands of years, following ways of life that respect the earth which you received as a legacy from past generations and are keeping for those yet to come. You have treated it as a gift of the Creator to be shared with others and to be cherished in harmony with all that exists, in profound fellowship with all living beings.[40]

At the Citadelle de Québec, he spoke of the constant concern of Indigenous Peoples for the environment "in fidelity to a harmonious vision of creation as an open book that teaches human beings to love the Creator and to live in symbiosis with other living creatures." He stressed the way that Indigenous traditions invite a long look into the future and the implications of the actions that we take today: "We need to be able to look, as the indigenous wisdom tradition teaches, seven generations ahead, and not to our immediate convenience, to the next elections, or the support of this or that lobby." In the midst of a frenzied pace of life, "we can learn much from this ability to listen attentively to God, to persons and to nature … In this regard, the values and teachings of the indigenous peoples are precious."[41]

In Iqaluit, Pope Francis spoke of the "beautiful and harmonious relationship between you and this land you inhabit," and he encouraged young Inuit to continue this tradition: "Care for the earth, care for your people, care for your history."[42] In this regard, Pope Francis encouraged the church and society in Canada to listen deeply to the wisdom of Indigenous ways of relating to and caring for the land and to learn from these ways for the sake of all of our futures.

POST-VISIT STATEMENT ON THE DOCTRINE OF DISCOVERY

Among the Truth and Reconciliation Commission's *Calls to Action* (2015), call 49 advocated that faith communities "repudiate concepts used to justify European sovereignty over Indigenous lands and peoples, such as the Doctrine of Discovery and *terra nullius*."[43] A coalition of Catholic entities in Canada, including the Canadian Conference of Catholic Bishops, responded to this call in 2016, at which time they asserted that "Indigenous people … should have been granted all fundamental human rights in the past as in the present," rejected the view "that the ancient principle of the first taker or discoverer, often described by the term *terra nullius*, could be applied to lands in the prior possession of Indigenous Peoples" and disavowed the idea that "the mere absence of European agricultural practices, technologies, or other aspects common to European culture, could justify the claiming of land as if it had no owner."[44] The statement was acknowledged by some Indigenous leaders but did not attract much attention, and in the lead-up to the papal visit and during the visit itself, there was a strong request for the Vatican to address the issue.

On 30 March 2023, the Holy See did so, with the joint statement on the Doctrine of Discovery issued by the Dicasteries for Culture and Education and for Promoting Integral Human Development.[45] On the same day as the Holy See's statement was issued, both the Canadian and American episcopal conferences released accompanying statements, each making reference to the possibility of hosting an academic symposium with Indigenous and non-Indigenous scholars to further the discussion in the North American context.[46]

There are six implications of this statement issued by the Holy See. First, it acknowledged the great suffering of Indigenous Peoples as a result of colonization, including "the expropriation of their lands" and policies of forced assimilation "intended to eliminate their indigenous cultures."[47] Second, it affirmed the rights and dignity of Indigenous Peoples, summoned people to walk side by side with them, called for the abandonment of an enduring colonizing mentality, and recommitted the Catholic Church "to accompany indigenous peoples and to foster efforts aimed at promoting reconciliation and healing."[48] Third, it stressed that the Catholic Church "repudiates those concepts that fail to recognize the inherent human rights of indigenous peoples, including what has become known as the legal and political 'doctrine of discovery.'"[49] Here, the document addressed legal concepts debated starting in the sixteenth century and in places legally enshrined in the nineteenth century, "according to which the discovery of lands by settlers granted an exclusive right to extinguish, either by purchase or conquest, the title to or possession of those lands by indigenous peoples."[50] Fourth, it acknowledged that papal bulls such as *Dum Diversas* (1452), *Romanus Pontifex* (1455), and *Inter Caetera* (1493) "did not adequately reflect the equal dignity and rights of indigenous peoples" and that their contents "were manipulated for political purposes by competing colonial powers in order to justify immoral acts against indigenous peoples that were carried out, at times, without opposition from ecclesiastical authorities."[51] Here, it asked for pardon and committed the church never again "to be infected by the idea that one culture is superior to others, or that it is legitimate to employ ways of coercing others."[52] Fifth, it clarified that the papal bulls in question were never understood as a doctrine in the Catholic sense, as these documents were political in nature and not expressions of Catholic faith,[53] and it pointed to the subsequent history of papal statements upholding the rights of Indigenous

Peoples, dating back to *Sublimis Deus* (1537). And, finally, it called for the implementation of principles found in the United Nations Declaration on the Rights of Indigenous Peoples (2007) as a means to improve their living conditions, protect their rights, and "facilitate their development in a way that respects their identity, language and culture."[54]

The response to the Holy See's statement was largely positive, as it was seen by many as a good step in the long walk of reconciliation. But media reports tended to miss key nuances of the document, frequently blurring or missing altogether the distinction between legal and ecclesial usage of the term "doctrine." On the one hand, the Holy See document wanted to acknowledge and apologize for aspects of ecclesial support for a colonizing enterprise with assimilation policies that deeply wounded and continue to hurt Indigenous people. On the other hand, it wanted to clarify that these documents did not define church doctrine, as they were not authoritative teachings about Christian faith but instead deeply problematic directives from popes to colonizing powers that were used to justify colonial expansion and exploitation. So the Holy See's text repudiates the *legal* Doctrine of Discovery, shares how the instruction in the papal bulls in question shifted toward the recognition of Indigenous rights beginning in 1537, and expresses the church's solidarity with the Indigenous pursuit of justice.

Planning has begun on a symposium or series of symposia on the subject of the Doctrine of Discovery, where Indigenous and non-Indigenous historians and legal scholars can hopefully pursue the topic further.

CONCLUSION

When Pope Francis returned to Rome and spoke of his visit to Canada, he commented on the pain that he felt in hearing from elderly in Iqaluit "who had lost their children and did not know what had become of them, due to this policy of assimilation." He added, "It was a very painful moment, but one we had to face: we must own up to our mistakes, to our sins."[55] The papal apology was an attempt to do that.

Pope Francis's words of apology did not meet every request or expectation from survivors and Indigenous communities. For some, it did not say enough. For others, it brought healing. For still others, it was a step along the way but one that needs to be made real through concrete actions, with solidarity being expressed in a way that builds relationships and restores trust. One survivor I have had the privilege of working with, Ted Quewezance of Keeseekoose First Nation in Saskatchewan, has frequently said that each survivor will need to make a decision about whether or not to accept the papal apology and that all survivors are on their own healing journey.

The motto of the papal visit was "Walking Together," which pointed to a new way for the church to be in relationship with Indigenous Peoples, a way characterized by respect, dialogue, solidarity, and the building of right relationships. While leaving the Cathedral-Basilica of Notre-Dame de Québec, Pope Francis was asked whether he wanted to write something in the visitors' book. He agreed to do so, and wrote, "Marcher ensemble, ce n'est pas facile, mais c'est possible" (It is not easy to walk together, but it is possible). That is the great invitation placed before both church and society in Canada as we live out the days after the apology.

NOTES

1 Truth and Reconciliation Commission of Canada, *Calls to Action* (2015), no. 58, https://www2.gov.bc.ca/assets/gov/british-columbians-our-governments/indigenous-people/aboriginal-peoples-documents/calls_to_action_english2.pdf: "We call upon the Pope to issue an apology to Survivors, their families, and communities for the Roman Catholic Church's role in the spiritual, cultural, emotional, physical, and sexual abuse of First Nations, Inuit, and Métis children in Catholic-run residential schools."

2 This phrase was coined by Chief Cadmus Delorme of Cowessess First Nation, Saskatchewan. Chief Cadmus Delorme and Archbishop Donald Bolen, "The Day After the Apology – A New Way of Walking Together," video, 19 October 2022, https://cpco.on.ca/CPCO/Event_Display.aspx?EventKey=VIRTCONF22.

3 Vatican, "Apostolic Journey of His Holiness Pope Francis to Canada, 24–30 July 2022," 23 June 2022, https://www.vatican.va/content/francesco/en/travels/2022/outside/documents/canada-2022.html. This document includes links to all papal addresses, homilies, and other public remarks related to the pope's visit.

4 Pope Francis, "Angelus," 17 July 2022, https://www.vatican.va/content/francesco/en/angelus/2022/documents/20220717-angelus.html.

5 Pope Francis, "Address of His Holiness: Maskwacis," 25 July 2022, https://www.vatican.va/content/francesco/en/speeches/2022/july/documents/20220725-popolazioniindigene-canada.html.

6 Pope Francis, "Homily of His Holiness: Basilica of Notre Dame de Québec," 28 July 2022, https://www.vatican.va/content/francesco/en/homilies/2022/documents/20220728-omelia-vespri-quebec.html.

7 Pope Francis, "Address of His Holiness: Maskwacis."

8 Pope Francis, "Address of His Holiness: Sacred Heart Church at Edmonton," 25 July 2022, https://www.vatican.va/content/francesco/en/speeches/2022/july/documents/20220725-incontroedmonton-canada.html.

9 Quoted in Antonio Spadaro, "Pope Francis Discusses Traditionalism, Liturgy Wars and Synodality with Jesuits in Canada," *America Magazine*, 4 August 2022, https://www.americamagazine.org/faith/2022/08/04/pope-francis-jesuits-canada-243481.

10 Pope Francis, "Address of His Holiness: Citadelle de Québec," 27 July 2022, https://www.vatican.va/content/francesco/en/speeches/2022/july/documents/20220727-autorita-canada.html, quoting Pope Francis, *Querida Amazonia*, 2 February 2020, para. 16, https://www.vatican.va/content/francesco/en/apost_exhortations/documents/papa-francesco_esortazione-ap_20200202_querida-amazonia.html.

11 Pope Francis, "Address of His Holiness: Primary School in Iqaluit," 29 July 2022, https://www.vatican.va/content/francesco/en/speeches/2022/july/documents/20220729-giovani-anziani-iqaluit.html.

12 Pope Francis, "Homily of His Holiness: Basilica."

13 Pope Francis, "Address of His Holiness Pope Francis: Clementine Hall," 1 April 2022, https://www.vatican.va/content/francesco/en/speeches/2022/april/documents/20220401-popoli-indigeni-canada.html.

14 Pope Francis, "Address of His Holiness: Maskwacis."

15 Pope Francis, "Address of His Holiness: Maskwacis."
16 Pope Francis, "Address of His Holiness: Maskwacis."
17 Pope Francis, "Homily of the Holy Father: Lac Ste. Anne," 26 July 2022, https://www.vatican.va/content/francesco/en/homilies/2022/documents/20220726-omelia-lacsteanne-canada.html.
18 Pope Francis, "Homily of the Holy Father: Lac Ste. Anne."
19 Pope Francis, "Address of His Holiness: Sacred Heart Church."
20 Pope Francis, "Address of His Holiness: Sacred Heart Church."
21 Truth and Reconciliation Commission of Canada, *Honouring the Truth, Reconciling for the Future: Summary of the Final Report of the Truth and Reconciliation Commission of Canada* (2015), 224, https://ehprnh2mwo3.exactdn.com/wp-content/uploads/2021/01/Executive_Summary_English_Web.pdf.
22 Pope Francis, "Address of His Holiness Pope Francis: Clementine Hall."
23 Pope Francis, "Address of His Holiness: Maskwacis," quoting Pope Francis, "Letters of His Holiness Pope Francis to the People of God," 20 August 2018, https://www.vatican.va/content/francesco/en/letters/2018/documents/papa-francesco_20180820_lettera-popolo-didio.html.
24 Pope Francis, "Address of His Holiness: Sacred Heart Church."
25 Pope Francis, "Address of His Holiness Pope Francis: Clementine Hall."
26 Pope Francis, "Address of His Holiness: Maskwacis."
27 Pope Francis, "Greeting of the Holy Father: Archbishop's Residence in Québec," 29 July 2022, https://www.vatican.va/content/francesco/en/speeches/2022/july/documents/20220729-delegazione-indigeni-quebec.html.
28 United Nations General Assembly, United Nations Declaration on the Rights of Indigenous Peoples (2007), https://www.un.org/development/desa/indigenouspeoples/wp-content/uploads/sites/19/2018/11/UNDRIP_E_web.pdf.
29 Pope Francis, "Address of His Holiness: Citadelle de Québec."
30 Call no. 48 of the Truth and Reconciliation Commission's *Calls to Action* (2015) advocates that the churches adopt the UN declaration "as a framework for reconciliation."

31 Pope Francis, "Homily of the Holy Father: Commonwealth Stadium in Edmonton," 26 July 2022, https://www.vatican.va/content/francesco/en/homilies/2022/documents/20220726-omelia-edmonton-canada.html.
32 Pope Francis, "Address of His Holiness: Maskwacis."
33 Pope Francis, "Homily of the Holy Father: Lac Ste. Anne."
34 Pope Francis, "Address of His Holiness: Citadelle de Québec."
35 Pope Francis, "Address of His Holiness: Primary School in Iqaluit."
36 Pope Francis, "General Audience: Paul VI Audience Hall," 3 August 2022, https://www.vatican.va/content/francesco/en/audiences/2022/documents/20220803-udienza-generale.html.
37 Pope Francis, "Address of His Holiness: Maskwacis."
38 Pope Francis, *Laudato Si'*, 24 May 2015, para. 146, https://www.vatican.va/content/francesco/es/encyclicals/documents/papa-francesco_20150524_enciclica-laudato-si.html.
39 Pope Francis, *Querida Amazonia*, 2 February 2020, para. 71, https://www.vatican.va/content/francesco/en/apost_exhortations/documents/papa-francesco_esortazione-ap_20200202_querida-amazonia.html.
40 Pope Francis, "Address of His Holiness: Maskwacis."
41 Pope Francis, "Address of His Holiness: Citadelle de Québec."
42 Pope Francis, "Address of His Holiness: Primary School in Iqaluit."
43 Truth and Reconciliation Commission, *Calls to Action*, no. 49.
44 Canadian Conference of Catholic Bishops, Canadian Catholic Aboriginal Council, Canadian Religious Conference, and Canadian Catholic Organization for Development and Peace, "The 'Doctrine of Discovery' and *Terra Nullius*: A Catholic Response," 19 March 2016, https://www.cccb.ca/wp-content/uploads/2017/11/catholic-response-to-doctrine-of-discovery-and-tn.pdf.
45 Holy See Press Office, "Joint Statement of the Dicasteries for Culture and Education and for Promoting Integral Human Development on the 'Doctrine of Discovery,'" 30 March 2023, https://press.vatican.va/content/salastampa/it/bollettino/pubblico/2023/03/30/0238/00515.html.
46 Canadian Conference of Catholic Bishops, "Statement by the Permanent Council of the Canadian Conference of Catholic Bishops on the Joint

Statement of the Dicastery for Culture and Education and the Dicastery for Promoting Integral Human Development on the 'Doctrine of Discovery,'" 30 March 2023, https://www.cccb.ca/letter/statement-by-the-permanent-council-of-the-canadian-conference-of-catholic-bishops-on-the-joint-statement-of-the-dicastery-for-culture-and-education-and-the-dicastery-for-promoting-integral-human-deve/; United States Conference of Catholic Bishops, "USCCB Statement on 'Doctrine of Discovery,'" 30 March 2023, https://www.usccb.org/news/2023/usccb-statement-doctrine-discovery.

47 Holy See Press Office, "Joint Statement of the Dicasteries," para. 4.

48 Holy See Press Office, "Joint Statement of the Dicasteries," para. 4.

49 Holy See Press Office, "Joint Statement of the Dicasteries," para. 7.

50 Holy See Press Office, "Joint Statement of the Dicasteries," para. 5.

51 Holy See Press Office, "Joint Statement of the Dicasteries," para. 6.

52 Holy See Press Office, "Joint Statement of the Dicasteries," para. 6.

53 Holy See Press Office, "Joint Statement of the Dicasteries," para. 6.

54 Holy See Press Office, "Joint Statement of the Dicasteries," para. 9.

55 Pope Francis, "General Audience."

2

Possibility and Impasse
The Authenticity of Pope Francis and the Messages Communicated by the Actions of the Catholic Church

Christine Jamieson

INTRODUCTION

In 2022, there were two significant meetings between the Indigenous Peoples living in the territory of what is now called Canada and Pope Francis, the head of the Roman Catholic Church. In the spring of 2022, Indigenous people from Turtle Island[1] – First Nations, Métis, and Inuit delegates who were elders, knowledge keepers, residential school survivors, and youth – travelled from Canada to Rome to meet with the pope in his territory. The meetings were both public and private. There were times when Pope Francis met face-to-face with residential school survivors and times when the gatherings were open to all visitors, including media. On the final day of the visit, 1 April 2022, the pope apologized for the abuses that Indigenous Peoples of Turtle Island suffered at the hands of members of the Catholic Church. Among the words that he uttered on that last day were the following: "For the deplorable conduct of these members of the Catholic Church,[2] I ask for God's forgiveness and I want to say to you with all my heart: I am very sorry."[3] A few months later, in July 2022,

Pope Francis travelled to Canada to meet with residential school survivors, their families, and communities. It was truly significant that the pope came to Turtle Island and apologized on this land, in this place that is home to over 630 First Nation communities, eight main Inuit groups, and the Métis Nation. Among these peoples, approximately 80,000 residential school survivors are still alive today.

Looking at these visits from the Ojibway-Anishinabe tradition, we might consider both encounters as instances of entering one another's lodges, an effort to come to understand each other's way of being and acting in the world. Don McCaskill and Jerry Fontaine explain the significance of entering one another's lodge this way:

> Bin-di-go-daa-di-win (To enter one another's lodge) is a process of coming together in such a way that the parties put aside their biases and enter into an agreement as to how to live together. Importantly, it entails a willingness for both parties to acquire a degree of understanding of the other's i-nah-di-zi-win (ontology), nah-nahn-gah-dah-wayn-ji-gay-win (epistemology), and bish-kayn-di-ji-gay-win (pedagogy). Inherent in the process is participating in a ceremony such as a Talking Circle, the exchange of gifts, and a Pipe Ceremony to arrive at some mutually agreed form of accommodation – that is, reconciliation.[4]

During his visit to Turtle Island, Pope Francis met with many residential school survivors, doing so again both publicly and privately. He listened, and on several occasions during his journey, he apologized.[5] Many residential school survivors were deeply moved by the pope's words, and many were grateful and felt that the remarks constituted part of their long journey to healing.

However, another dimension of the events surrounding Pope Francis's visit to Turtle Island comprised actions that were highly inappropriate given that the focus of the visit was on residential school survivors and their families. In concert with the possibility of the good relations generated by the pope himself, an impasse emerged during very public events of the Catholic Church that showed it continuing to exhibit itself in a hierarchical manner, potentially triggering the very wounds that wrought so much pain and suffering for residential school survivors and their families in the first place. I refer, in particular, to two large Masses – one at Edmonton in Alberta and the other at Sainte-Anne-de-Beaupré in Quebec – where cardinals, bishops, and priests took centre stage, with Indigenous Peoples relegated to the back seats.

The pope's words can be weighed against actions. Amid public and private apologies, we saw public and private demonstrations of the sidelining of Indigenous presence and importance. Each part of this dialectic between possibility and impasse needs exploration. This chapter probes this stark contrast by acknowledging and exploring Pope Francis's desire to truly encounter residential school survivors and to communicate his sincere apology. The chapter also offers a critique of the Catholic Church's problematic and exclusive hierarchical tradition.

POSSIBILITY: THE FACE-TO-FACE ENCOUNTER AND MOVING TOWARD JUSTICE

It is possible to think of Pope Francis as a pilgrim, one who carried on his shoulders the weight of the Catholic Church, including the shadow, the shame, and the horrific side of the church, as he travelled to Canada on what he called his "penitential pilgrimage."[6] This human being, not only because of what he represented but also because of who he was as a person, came to Canada to encounter residential school survivors and to apologize. Here, we are reminded of the "culture of encounter" about which Pope Francis often spoke. For example, in a September 2016 homily delivered during a Mass at Domus Sanctae Marthae, his residence in Rome, he spoke of

> an invitation to work for "the culture of encounter," in a simple way, "as Jesus did": not just seeing, but looking; not just hearing, but listening; not just passing people by, but stopping with them; not just

> saying "what a shame, poor people!," but allowing yourself to be moved with compassion; "and then to draw near, to touch and to say: 'Do not weep' and to give at least a drop of life."[7]

Pope Francis's words and actions both at the meetings with the delegation that travelled to Rome in March 2022 and at the meetings with residential school survivors during his visit to Canada in July 2022 constituted a true encounter. Full of joy and full of sorrow, these encounters were in part healing, but because of other actions taken during the visit, they also triggered deep wounds from a traumatic past.

It seems to me that in the experiences and testimonies of survivors who met with Pope Francis, both in Rome and during his week-long visit to Turtle Island, encounter was necessarily prior to the justice that was demanded.[8] One can witness this sequence in the responses to Pope Francis's apology. Chief Wilton Littlechild, a commissioner of the Truth and Reconciliation Commission of Canada, said that he

> felt a swell of emotions and tears in his eyes as he heard Pope Francis apologize at the Vatican on Friday for the Roman Catholic Church's role in residential schools.
>
> The words came on the chief's 78th birthday. It was especially meaningful, he said, because during the 14 years he attended residential school as a child in Alberta, he was not allowed to celebrate [his birthday].
>
> "I hoped for it. I prayed for it. I dreamt for it," he said. "But I never expected to live and see and feel it."[9]

Similarly, eighty-five-year-old Métis elder Angie Crerar, with tears streaming down her face, said that "she could see that Francis spoke with sincerity. 'My heart is so full I can hardly speak.'"[10] Dr Cora Voyageur, a professor in the Department of Sociology at the University of Calgary and a residential school survivor, travelled to Maskwacis to hear Pope Francis's apology. She made the following observation: "It was a very long and emotional day. There were mixed emotions expressed by people in the crowd with some sobbing, while others were elated. I was thankful for the traditional healing centres that provided an opportunity to cleanse ourselves with smudges and cedar brushing."[11] Chief Greg Desjarlais of Frog Lake First Nation felt positive about the pope's apology: "I felt the apology to be sincere. I felt the pope really did some homework. He dug in and made it as meaningful as he can."[12]

French philosopher Emmanuel Levinas speaks of ethics as emerging when one encounters the face of another.[13] Levinas literally means the human face of the other, another human being with whom we come face to face. Ethics, for Levinas, is first of all the responsibility to which we are called in encountering the face of another. As Levinas suggests, the face of the other escapes categorization. "The face is present in its refusal to be contained. In this sense it cannot be comprehended, that is, encompassed."[14] In its immediacy, the face of the other captures me and calls me to responsibility. "The Other becomes my neighbour precisely through the way the face summons me, calls for me, begs for me, and in so doing recalls my responsibility, and calls me into question."[15] This is the danger of truly encountering another. It takes courage because in that encounter we are reminded of our unfathomable responsibility for the other and we – our lives and our actions – are called into question. It points to our intrinsic relationality.

Following Levinas's philosophy, we human beings are relational before we are individual. Our individuality emerges from our relations with others – we are born into a culture, a language, a family long before our sense of self emerges. Even more radically, drawing on the work of Levinas, Sara E. Roberts writes, "It is not the case that I am first a self, who afterwards takes on responsibilities, but rather my unique selfhood enters the picture in the first place when I am accused, called, blamed, and held responsible by the other."[16] Not only does our sense of self emerge from our original relationality, but our "asymmetrical responsibility" for the other also emerges in our face-to-face encounter with the other.[17] Levinas contends that prior to our ability to ground ourselves in our subjectivity, we have already been summoned by the other to respond. "Indeed, for Levinas, responsibility could not possibly arise from something in me; he argues that the self first arises in that responsibility. Thus, rather than having its source in me, this responsibility draws its authority solely from the face of the other before me, experienced as a demand or a call for help."[18] Levinas writes: "The word *I* means *here I am*, answering for everything and for everyone."[19]

Given this radical call to responsibility in the face-to-face encounter, how might justice play out, and how might it be possible? For Levinas, justice must move beyond the encounter with one other who calls me to be responsible for that person. It necessarily involves more than one other. Therefore, if I am called to responsibility by the face of the other, how can I bring about justice for all? For Levinas, this call to responsibility precedes justice, but it does not eradicate the need for justice: "The interpersonal relation I establish with the Other, I must also establish with other men; there is thus a necessity to moderate this privilege of the Other; from whence comes justice."[20] Justice comes later when we realize that there are additional others also demanding our response. Again, "all human experience is in some ways founded on a primordial ethical relation in which the Self acknowledges its responsibility for the Other,"[21] with the world we inhabit exposing us to more than one other. It is precisely this reality of many others that compels us "to develop principles of justice that help us adjudicate between these responsibilities" as "mechanisms for judging generosity and threat, for protecting people generally from those who threaten them with violence in various ways, and for organizing life to help and protect all."[22] That is how Levinas understands justice. Justice is vitally important, but it must "always be held in check by the initial interpersonal relation."[23]

Through the lens of Levinas's insights, it is valuable to explore Pope Francis's insistence on a culture of encounter and how it manifested in his concrete encounters with Indigenous survivors of residential schools. Indigenous people living in Canada who went through the residential school experience wanted Pope Francis to come to Canada. It was not enough that their representatives had travelled to Rome and heard his apology there. They wanted him to come to Turtle Island. Employing the

Ojibway-Anishinabe tradition, the survivors wanted Pope Francis to apologize in their territory and in their lodge. In the language of Levinas, they wanted to "see" his face and call him to responsibility in his encounter with their suffering. The significance of these encounters is that they were truly ethical, as Levinas so profoundly explains this phenomenon. Pope Francis looked at each survivor he came face to face with and was responsible for each one. In the context of his pilgrimage of penance, he carried and lived this responsibility each time he met a survivor.

Yet the overwhelming number of Indigenous people who suffered from the residential school experience made Pope Francis's expression of his unfathomable responsibility for all these others unattainable. This was the case not only because of Pope Francis's frailty, evident during his visit to Turtle Island, but even more so because of the sheer impossibility of meeting all who had suffered at the hands of members of the Catholic Church. The importance of justice for all emerges precisely in the midst of the impossible call to responsibility not only for the other(s) the pope encountered but also for all the others he could not personally encounter. Two specific examples highlight a means of addressing this chasm between responsibility and need, and both have to do with justice: justice as action and justice as meaning.

Some commentators have noted the justice inherent in the concrete actions that have already been taken by the Catholic Church since Indigenous people's encounters with Pope Francis. Already, we have seen one example in the "Joint Statement of the Dicasteries for Culture and Education and for Promoting Integral Human Development on the 'Doctrine of Discovery'" (2023).[24] Many Indigenous people in Canada were very happy that the joint statement came out. Many connected it to the pope's visit the previous summer, regarding it as an indication that Pope Francis had acted on the request to rescind the Doctrine of Discovery. In fact, this request was the most prominent one made by residential school survivors.[25] As an act, the statement is important. Words are important, and in the statement, we have the Catholic Church, "in no uncertain terms," repudiating "those concepts that fail to recognize the inherent human rights of indigenous peoples, including what has become known as the legal and political 'doctrine of discovery.'"[26] The joint statement acknowledges that "certain scholars have argued that the basis of the aforementioned 'doctrine' is to be found in several papal documents, such as the Bulls *Dum Diversas* (1452), *Romanus Pontifex* (1455) and *Inter Caetera* (1493)."[27]

The statement has a broader focus beyond the Doctrine of Discovery. It addresses underlying assumptions from the time of the writing of the papal bulls, attitudes that continue to exist. Rev. David McCallum, executive director of the Program for Discerning Leadership, based in Rome, expresses this well: "The statement repudiates the very mindsets and worldview that gave rise to the original papal bulls … It renounces the mindset of cultural or racial superiority which allowed for that objectification or subjection of people, and strongly condemns any attitudes or actions that threaten or damage the dignity of the human person."[28] In a *Globe and Mail* article, former Assembly of First Nations national chief RoseAnne Archibald stated, "This is a step in the right direction, but this is a thousand-mile journey. These issues with the doctrine go back 500 years. To undo the damage they have caused will take time."[29] With Archibald, I can neither totally applaud the joint statement nor totally criticize it. I must see it as a step on a long journey – one that may reimagine a different future while overturning the Doctrine of Discovery at every level that it has caused harm. That would be the road to justice, a justice that is necessarily always in progress.

Beyond the face-to-face encounter, justice was also manifested in the words that Pope Francis spoke not only to the immediate other but also to all residential survivors who sought some form of healing through the pope's pilgrimage of penance. As Levinas states, "Justice remains justice only in a society where there is no distinction between those close and those far off, but in which there also remains the impossibility of passing by the closest."[30] Roberts explains Levinas's statement this way: "My relationship with the other in proximity gives meaning to my relationship to all others as 'citizens' or abstract members of a moral community."[31] At different levels, meaning was constituted. Even though Pope Francis's encounters with residential school survivors emphasized the face-to-face encounters that took place in these meetings, the pope said that he intended the *meaning* of the words and actions to go beyond these specific encounters. In other words, the meaning of the apologies exceeded the small group that encountered Pope Francis during his time in Canada and during the Indigenous delegates' visit to Rome. It reached out to many residential school survivors across Canada and perhaps even beyond Canada.

The significance and power of his apologies are important to note. There is a force behind such official words that can heal. In this sense – that of a speech-act – the apologies were not descriptive but creative. They created an act. It was an action that was not merely acknowledged for its truth value – that is, as an apology that had been uttered. Rather, the utterance itself constituted an action – that of apologizing. This effect, in part, explains the power behind the words and the emotionally charged responses to them. The reverberations of Pope Francis's speech acts, the acts of apologizing, went well beyond the small number of Indigenous Peoples who witnessed them in person. Beyond the weight of a speech act, I think that the power of the apology had something to do with what Bernard Lonergan identifies as "incarnate meaning."[32]

Lonergan identifies different "carriers of meaning," or different ways that meaning is embodied.[33] Here, the focus is on incarnate meaning – heart speaking to heart. Incarnate meaning "is the meaning of a person, of his way of life, of his words, or of his deeds. It may be his meaning for just one other person, or for a small group, or for a whole national, or social, or cultural, or religious tradition."[34] Thinking about incarnate meaning in relation to the meetings between Indigenous survivors and Pope Francis helps one to understand both the intensity and the intended outreach of the apologies. Although the encounter was face-to-face, the incarnate meaning of Pope Francis's words to Indigenous survivors of residential schools and their families allowed for a broadening of the meaning and impact of the apologies. This effect explains why the apologies spoke to so many survivors even though they were physically present neither in the various places in Canada that the pope visited nor in Rome when the delegation visited the pope. Although encounter demands the face-to-face relation, the incarnate meaning of Pope Francis's apologies allowed his words to move beyond the immediacy of those present to the much larger number of survivors watching and listening from their own territories. Beyond his office as pope, it was clearly Pope Francis who was speaking from the heart. In this sense, his apologies conveyed a meaning that came from the person he was, the life he had lived, the words he had spoken, and the deeds he had done. As stated by Natan Obed, president of Inuit Tapiriit Kanatami, "Behind the coverups, behind the indifference of over 100 years, behind the lies, behind the lack of justice, this pope – Pope Francis – decided to go right through it and decided to speak words the First Nations, Inuit and Métis have been longing to hear for decades."[35]

IMPASSE: CLASSICISM VERSUS HISTORICAL CONSCIOUSNESS

Despite witnessing the profound encounters between Pope Francis and residential school survivors as well as the acts of intentional and restorative justice that were subsequently undertaken by the Catholic Church, it is striking to note the large clerical presence during the Eucharist both at Edmonton and at Sainte-Anne-de-Beaupré. I note this presence because during these celebrations, it was almost possible to forget the purpose and focus of the pope's visit. The absence of Indigenous survivors in the procession and sitting in the front seats was startling. The absence of Indigenous symbols and ceremonies on the altar and during the service was disheartening. This "business as usual" display seemed to contradict everything Pope Francis had come to communicate to residential school survivors.

Why, for instance, was a smudging ceremony not undertaken instead of the intense display of incense purifying the altar and those on the altar? Certainly, that would have been an amazing symbolic gesture in line with the purpose and goal of Pope Francis's pilgrimage of penance. Although the pope sincerely sought reconciliation, this reconciliation did not seem to touch (or even to be in mind during) these particular forms of celebration of the Eucharist, forms that themselves emerge from a particular culture in history. At these moments, the clash of cultures was palpable. Whatever Pope Francis's intent and his words, Indigenous ways of being and doing were either ignored or dismissed in the practical working out of these very public manifestations of what it means to be Catholic. And it was precisely this clash of cultures that former Truth and Reconciliation Commission chair Murray Sinclair and others refer to when they say that the Catholic Church has not gone far enough.[36]

These high-profile discrepancies between what is said and what is done show a tension within the Catholic Church, one reflected in the papal visit. The tension is between what Lonergan calls "classicism" and "historical consciousness," or the recognition that all human beings and all cultures are historically situated. With the former, "culture was understood normatively, in terms of a single ideal that we suppose all women and men aspired towards achieving," and with the latter, "we regard cultures empirically, as presenting different ways of organizing life, even with its own set of ideals."[37] Achiel Peelman, in his book *Christ Is a Native American* (2006), explores the notion of inculturation, shedding light on the contradiction that the Roman Catholic Church displayed at the two Eucharists during the pope's visit:

> Inculturation, in fact, is something that happens between the gospel itself (the seed) and the receiving culture (the soil). The role of the sower, the missionary church, remains very important, but is secondary with respect to the people who receive the gospel. The role of the receiving people or culture is primordial. It is "on its own," the parable says, that the land produces fruit. But the main role, in this process, belongs to the gospel itself. Jesus, the Christ, is himself the main actor in the inculturation process, because he IS the Word proclaimed by the church and received by peoples. He IS the way, the truth and the light.[38]

Simply put, inculturation was not on display during the Eucharists at Edmonton and at Sainte-Anne-de-Beaupré. On display instead was one particular culture – in fact, the particular culture that had played a significant role in operating the residential schools and in what the Truth and Reconciliation Commission called a "cultural genocide."[39] The discrepancy between word and public symbol seems to indicate that however sincere the pope's words and actions, the Catholic Church in Canada as an institution has not yet adopted a framework that can come to terms with its role in the spiritual, sexual, cultural, emotional, and physical abuse suffered by Indigenous children attending residential schools or with the systemic problem that the schools embodied as instruments appointed by the state and the church for the erasure of Indigenous culture on Turtle Island. Unfortunately, this lack of sensitivity to Indigenous culture was on display in the celebrations of the Eucharist, where the presence of cardinals, bishops, and clergy in the first rows at times obscured the fact that the visit was meant to be an encounter with survivors and Indigenous communities.

As many said during the pope's visit, healing must take place not only between but also within both parties. Healing for Indigenous survivors will constitute both an interior and an exterior journey. Healing within the Catholic Church must constitute a reappropriation of truth and value in the face of the evil that it has been part of over many centuries. Part of this evil is the privileging of a particular cultural construction and its not-so-subtle equation with the church's work and message, an evil enacted to the detriment of other forms of culture that might equally be sites of incarnation.

CONCLUSION

The goal of this chapter is not to be overly critical of the Catholic Church, many of whose leaders worked hard to bring about the important visits between Pope Francis and Indigenous survivors of residential schools. These leaders addressed call 58 of the Truth and Reconciliation Commission's *Calls to Action* (2015) by appealing to the pope to come to Canada and apologize on this land and by working hard to make the visits happen.[40] Rather, the goal is to try not only to point out and understand the possibilities that emerged during and after the pope's visit but also to recognize and acknowledge a disconnect that happened.

Certainly, the visit brought about face-to-face encounters between Pope Francis and Indigenous survivors of residential schools, their families, and their communities. These encounters were vital to the healing process of many. These encounters brought the pope directly into relation with others for whom he bore enormous responsibility. He bore this responsibility in a brave and humble manner. Although reactions to the pope's visit were mixed, there was no doubt that many were grateful for his sincere and heartfelt apologies.

The disconnect evident in the spectacle that characterized the large public Masses at Edmonton and at Sainte-Anne-de-Beaupré represented an unfortunate message concerning the relations between Indigenous survivors of residential schools – indeed, all Indigenous Peoples on Turtle Island – and the Catholic Church. This spectacle included the way that the hierarchy of the Roman Catholic Church was on display both in the opening procession and on the altar during the Masses. How different the message might have been if Indigenous survivors of residential schools, their families, and their community members had been first in the procession and had surrounded the pope on the altar during the Masses. I acknowledge that there was some presence of Indigenous Peoples during the ceremonies. However, compared to the massive presence of cardinals, bishops, and priests and given the placement of the different groups, these moments were hardly prominent. I believe that we cannot understate the negative impact of the symbolism of this display. In my view, it symbolizes an impasse that still haunts the Catholic Church and prevents the deep healing that must take place both for Indigenous Peoples who have suffered so terribly at the hands of the Catholic Church and for the church itself – its members and the institution.

NOTES

A small part of this chapter was taken from my article "Pope Francis's Apology: Encounter and Meaning," *Journal of Moral Theology* 12, no. 1 (2023): 63–71. I thank Matthew R. Anderson for reviewing this chapter and offering helpful feedback.

1 Turtle Island is the name that many Indigenous Peoples call Canada and all of North America.

2 It is important to acknowledge that many are critical that this apology, like the others that followed when Pope Francis visited Canada, singled out "members" of the Catholic Church rather than acknowledging the role that the institution itself had played in the residential school system and the abuses. There was also criticism that he acknowledged physical, verbal, psychological, and spiritual abuse but said nothing about the sexual abuse that was suffered.

3 Pope Francis, "Address of His Holiness Pope Francis: Clementine Hall," 1 April 2022, https://www.vatican.va/content/francesco/en/speeches/2022/april/documents/20220401-popoli-indigeni-canada.html.

4 Don McCaskill and Jerry Fontaine, *Di-Bayn-Di-Zi-Win: To Own Ourselves* (Toronto: Dundurn, 2022), 19.

5 See Pope Francis, "Address of His Holiness: Maskwacis," 25 July 2022, https://www.vatican.va/content/francesco/en/speeches/2022/july/documents/20220725-popolazioniindigene-canada.html; Pope Francis, "Address of His Holiness: Citadelle de Québec," 27 July 2022, https://www.vatican.va/content/francesco/en/speeches/2022/july/documents/20220727-autorita-canada.html; and Pope Francis, "Address of His Holiness: Primary School in Iqaluit," 29 July 2022, https://www.vatican.va/content/francesco/en/speeches/2022/july/documents/20220729-giovani-anziani-iqaluit.html. For transcripts of these apologies and others in several Indigenous languages, see Government of Canada, "Papal Apology for Residential Schools in Canada," n.d., https://www.rcaanc-cirnac.gc.ca/eng/1689770368923/1689770422117#sec2.

6 Pope Francis, "Angelus," 17 July 2022, https://www.vatican.va/content/francesco/en/angelus/2022/documents/20220717-angelus.html.

7 Pope Francis, "For a Culture of Encounter," 13 September 2016, quoted in *L'Osservatore Romano*, weekly ed. in English, no. 38, 23 September 2016, https://www.vatican.va/content/francesco/en/cotidie/2016/documents/papa-francesco-cotidie_20160913_for-a-culture-of-encounter.html.

8 The idea of the face-to-face encounter being prior to justice draws on the work of Emmanuel Levinas, particularly *Totality and Infinity: An Essay on Exteriority*, trans. Alphonso Lingis (Pittsburgh, PA: Duquesne University Press, 1969), and *Otherwise Than Being, or Beyond Essence*, trans. Alphonso Lingis (Pittsburgh, PA: Duquesne University Press, 1998).

9 Kelly Geraldine Malone, "'I prayed for it': Emotions, Tears as Pope Apologizes for Residential Schools," *Toronto Star*, 1 April 2022, https://www.thestar.com/news/canada/2022/04/01/indigenous-delegates-set-to-have-final-meeting-with-pope-francis-at-vatican.html.

10 Quoted in Malone, "'I prayed for it.'"

11 Quoted in Michelle Crossland, "UCalgary Residential School Survivor Shares Reactions from Pope's Apology," *UCalgary News*, 12 August 2022, https://ucalgary.ca/news/ucalgary-residential-school-survivor-shares-reactions-popes-apology.

12 Quoted in Canadian Press, "Pope Francis Apology: A Look at Reactions across Canada," *Global News*, 25 July 2022, https://globalnews.ca/news/9014362/pope-francis-apology-canada-reaction/.

13 See Levinas, *Totality and Infinity*, esp. sec. 3.B, titled "Ethics and the Face"; and Emmanuel Levinas, *Ethics and Infinity: Conversations with Philippe Nemo*, trans. Richard A. Cohen (Pittsburgh, PA: Duquesne University Press, 1984), esp. ch. 7, titled "The Face."

14 Levinas, *Totality and Infinity*, 194.

15 Emmanuel Levinas, "Ethics as First Philosophy," trans. Seán Hand and Michael Temple, in *The Levinas Reader*, ed. Seán Hand, 75–87 (Cambridge, MA: Blackwell, 1992), 83. As in the quotation cited here, Levinas and many of his commentators capitalize "Other" in order to point to the authority of those seen as the other to teach us who they are. It is a way of acknowledging the alterity of the other. Those situated as the other are beyond our ideas of them.

16 Sara E. Roberts, "Rethinking Justice: Levinas and Asymmetrical Responsibility," *Philosophy in the Contemporary World* 7, no. 1 (2000): 6.

17 Roberts, "Rethinking Justice."

18 Roberts, "Rethinking Justice," 6.

19 Levinas, *Otherwise Than Being*, 114, original emphasis.

20 Levinas, *Ethics and Infinity*, 90.

21 Joshua Shaw, "Justice in Emmanuel Levinas and John Rawls," *International Journal of Philosophical Studies* 28, no. 4 (2020): 472.

22 Ibid., 472.

23 Levinas, *Ethics and Infinity*, 90.

24 Holy See Press Office, "Joint Statement of the Dicasteries for Culture and Education and for Promoting Integral Human Development on the 'Doctrine of Discovery,'" 30 March 2023, https://press.vatican.va/content/salastampa/it/bollettino/pubblico/2023/03/30/0238/00515.html.

25 Examples of cautious optimism in response to the joint statement can be found in Nicole Winfield, "Indigenous Leaders Hope Vatican's Repudiation of Oppressive Colonial Concepts Leads to Real Change," CBC *News*, 30 March 2023, https://www.cbc.ca/news/canada/vatican-reject-discovery-doctrine-indigenous-demands-1.6795728. Notable are the words of Phil Fontaine, former national chief of the Assembly of First Nations in Canada: "The Holy Father promised that upon his return to Rome, they would begin work on a statement which was designed to allay the fears and concerns of many survivors and others concerned about the relationship between their Catholic Church and our people, and he did as he said he would do." However, many were critical of the joint statement, including Kenneth Deer, a member of the Haudenosaunee External Relations Committee, who said, "This seems to be more damage control by the Vatican, than sincere recognition of the role and responsibility to the church." Quoted in Nicky Taylor, "Vatican Relents on Papal Bulls," *Eastern Door*, 13 April 2023, https://easterndoor.com/2023/04/13/vatican-relents-on-papal-bulls/.

26 Holy See Press Office, "Joint Statement of the Dicasteries," para. 7.

27 Holy See Press Office, "Joint Statement of the Dicasteries," para. 5.

28 Quoted in Bill Chapelle, "The Vatican Repudiates 'Doctrine of Discovery,' Which Was Used to Justify Colonialism," NPR, 30 March 2023, https://www.npr.org/2023/03/30/1167056438/vatican-doctrine-of-discovery-colonialism-indigenous.

29 Quoted in Eric Reguly, "Vatican Formally Rejects Doctrine of Discovery That Allowed Colonial-Era Seizure of Indigenous Lands," *Globe and Mail*, 30 March 2023. https://www.theglobeandmail.com/world/article-doctrine-discovery-vatican-city/.

30 Emmanuel Levinas, "Peace and Proximity," in *Emmanuel Levinas: Basic Philosophical Writings*, ed. Adriaan Peperzak, Simon Critchley, and Robert Bernasconi, 161–70 (Indianapolis: Indiana University Press, 1996), 168, quoted in Roberts, "Rethinking Justice," 9.

31 Roberts, "Rethinking Justice," 9.

32 Bernard Lonergan, *Method in Theology* (Toronto: University of Toronto Press, 1971), 73.

33 The carriers of meaning – art, symbols, linguistic meaning, and incarnate meaning – are intersubjective. See Lonergan, *Method in Theology*, 57–73.

34 Lonergan, *Method in Theology*, 73.

35 Quoted in Malone, "'I prayed for it.'"

36 See Anishinaabe scholar Niigaan Sinclair's interview with his father, Murray Sinclair, in "CBC Radio's The House: TRC Calls to Action – What's Next?" CBC *News: The House*, 30 July 2022, https://www.cbc.ca/radio/thehouse/cbc-the-house-july-30-1.6536307.

37 Kenneth R. Melchin, "The Challenge of Historical Consciousness: Healing Divisions in the Church," *Lonergan Review* 7, no. 1 (2016): 87.

38 Achiel Peelman, *Christ Is a Native American* (Eugene, OR: Wipf and Stock, 2006), 92.

39 "For over a century, the central goals of Canada's Aboriginal policy were to eliminate Aboriginal governments; ignore Aboriginal rights; terminate the Treaties; and, through a process of assimilation, cause Aboriginal peoples to cease to exist as distinct legal, social, cultural, religious, and racial entities in Canada. The establishment and operation of residential schools were a central element of this policy, which can best be described as 'cultural genocide.'" Truth and Reconciliation Commission of Canada, *Honouring the Truth, Reconciling for the Future: Summary of the Final Report of the Truth and Reconciliation Commission of Canada* (2015), 1, https://ehprnh2mwo3.exactdn.com/wp-content/uploads/2021/01/Executive_Summary_English_Web.pdf.

40 Call 58 states, "We call upon the pope to issue an apology to Survivors, their families, and communities for the Roman Catholic Church's role in the spiritual, cultural, emotional, physical, and sexual abuse of First Nations, Inuit, and Métis children in Catholic-run residential schools. We call for that apology to be similar to the 2010 apology issued to Irish victims of abuse and to occur within one year of the issuing of this Report and to be delivered by the pope in Canada." Truth and Reconciliation Commission of Canada, *Calls to Action* (2015), no. 58, https://www2.gov.bc.ca/assets/gov/british-columbians-our-governments/indigenous-people/aboriginal-peoples-documents/calls_to_action_english2.pdf.

3

Bless You, Church, for You Have Sinned
An Ecclesiological Analysis of Papal Apologies and the Doctrine of Discovery

Annie Selak

INTRODUCTION

"The Pope Apologized" or similar headlines ran in newspapers throughout the world in July 2022[1] following what Pope Francis had called his "penitential pilgrimage" to Canada.[2] Although headlines may make his apology sound straightforward, ecclesial and papal apologies are far from clear. For what exactly is the pope apologizing? Is the pope claiming responsibility, apologizing on someone's behalf, or avoiding blame? Is the apology genuine? If so, what actions will result from this penance and conversion? These questions are important, and to address them, we must engage in an ecclesiological analysis of papal apologies.

This chapter's ecclesiological analysis looks at Pope Francis's apology at Maskwacis on 25 July 2022 during his penitential pilgrimage to Canada.[3] There are many similarities between this apology and other papal apologies, yet this apology is distinct due to its connection to prior meetings and its promise of future action. In this examination, I engage in a textual analysis of the apology statement and look at the significance of which words are included or left out. Pope Francis apologized for a wide range of actions, including the Catholic Church's colonizing mentality, acts of members of the church, and attitudes of indifference. However, he often placed a distance between the institutional church and the members of the church who perpetrated these offences.

Following this textual analysis, I look to the repudiation of the Doctrine of Discovery in connection with the papal apology.[4] Similar to Pope Francis's apology, the repudiation of the Doctrine of Discovery makes important forward progress, while still being permeated by a Eurocentric mentality that limits its authenticity. It speaks of the church as separate from Indigenous Peoples and, in the process, puts forth a narrow ecclesiology. Both of these theological statements are advances in reconciliation processes and envision an ecclesiology that is marked by justice, yet both also fall short of living into a truly just theological vision of the church.

Prior to this analysis, it is helpful to begin with some social locations. I am a white, cisgender woman. I am a Roman Catholic feminist theologian. I study ecclesiology and am attentive to issues of power and authority in the Catholic Church. I engage in this research at Georgetown University in Washington, DC, which is the homeland of the Nacotchtank and their descendants, the Piscataway Conoy people. Georgetown continues to benefit from the unpaid work and forced contributions of the 272 people who were enslaved by the Jesuits of the Maryland Province.[5]

PAPAL APOLOGIES

Theology of Apology

For most of church history, the idea of regarding the church as sinning or sinful, and therefore as needing to apologize for anything, was beyond comprehension. There was a sense that the church was holy and, by this virtue, was incapable of error. Or, if the church was seen as sinful, this trait was attributed to its members, as though the church as an institution could be considered without its members. The purity of the church's holiness was preserved by this false division of the church from its sinful members.

Prior to Pope Paul VI asking for the forgiveness of "separated brethren" at the Second Vatican Council in 1963, the last pope who had apologized was Pope Adrian VI in the early sixteenth century.[6] Over this 450-year period, ecclesial repentance was so far removed from the operative ecclesiology that Pope Gregory XVI in 1832 asserted that the church could not express repentance. Theologian Luigi Accotoli summarizes this ecclesial mindset: "To admit defect or stain in the Church could lead to the suggestion of a reform and since this would be very dangerous, it was felt necessary at all costs to avoid admitting any fault."[7] Reform was equated with danger for much of church history, but the world and the operative ecclesiology began to shift in the twentieth century. This understanding of holiness and sin changed in the theological paradigm shift of the Second Vatican Council, opening the door to ecclesial repentance in a new way.[8] Given the church's connection to widespread suffering in the context of world wars and the Shoah, theologians directed more attention to examining the relationship between sin and holiness. The church was holy, to be sure, but the church was also part of this world and participated in atrocities.

Ecclesiologist Brian P. Flanagan outlines several reasons for the new attention to sinfulness in the church, such as the need for the church to be honest about its past and actions, the threat of hypocrisy to the mission of the church, the need for fidelity to those impacted by the sins of the church, and the church's connection to preaching the Gospel, the good news of Jesus Christ.[9] Understanding the church as capable of sinning is a way of expressing its mission as aligned with those who are intentionally and historically marginalized. It is not just that a church capable of sinning is a theological possibility; rather, this recognition is necessary in understanding a church where sin occurs.

Ecclesial apologies defy standard norms of apologies, making theological investigations of papal apologies a rich topic. Typical apologies are directed from the perpetrator or aggressor to the victim. Ecclesial apologies, in contrast, often do not come from the direct aggressor but from the leader of the institution connected to the perpetrator(s). In the case at hand, Pope Francis was not involved in the creation or support of residential schools, yet he was not disconnected from this reality. Tradition in the Catholic Church places the leader of the church, the pope, in an important symbolic and concrete role of representing the past church along with the contemporary church. So, too, is Pope Leo XIV connected to this papal tradition.

In Catholic theology, because of the expansive nature of the term "church," it can refer simultaneously to the current expression of the people of God, to church hierarchy, and to institutions, as well as to these expressions throughout time and tradition. Even the Dogmatic Constitution of the Church, *Lumen Gentium* (1964), reflects the multiplicity of meanings of the term "church," referring to the mystery of church, the people of God, the hierarchy, laity, and the pilgrim church.[10] Although the many meanings of church can result in confusing conversations, they also attest to the way that the church can embody paradox. In the Catholic context, the church is marked by paradox, such as being sinful and holy, local and global, universal and particular. These are not contradictions but speak to the mystery of the church. The church is expressed in the here and now despite not being restricted to the here and now. In analyzing ecclesial apologies, this paradoxical nature of the church becomes especially important, for it addresses how the pope can speak to sins and errors that he did not personally perpetrate but to which he is connected by virtue of his role as leader of the church. The pope represents more than himself, and the church is more than one person. Consequently, the pope can speak to a collective harm and collective responsibility.

Whereas collective guilt may not be helpful, collective responsibility can be a tool of moral conversion. Jeremy M. Bergen argues that collective responsibility is necessary because of the enduring impact of structural sin on the church. He explains, "The structures of racism or colonialism are such that they blinded the church, especially those with the power to speak on behalf of the church, which as a result failed to form its members to avoid and oppose those sins."[11] Because the impact of colonialism and racism is enduring, repentance should not be confined to the past.

Significantly, collective understanding of the possibility of ecclesial apologies changed during the pontificate of John Paul II. In 1999, ahead of the Day of Pardon called by John Paul II in 2000, the International Theological Commission spoke about the need for public apologies: "And it is thus that the remembrance of scandals of the past can become an obstacle to the Church's witness today, and the recognition of the past faults of the Church's sons and daughters of yesterday can foster renewal and reconciliation in the present."[12] This statement affirms the connection between the church's past and its ability to credibly uphold its mission in the present. For example, the church's involvement with colonialism, enslavement of people, and other expressions of racism were accepted by the church at the time, yet this acceptance and even encouragement have an impact on the church's credibility today. Without repentance, the church can be seen as an extension of colonialism and racism rather than seen to be aligned with the mission of the Gospel and with advancing justice. Recognizing the "scandals of the past" and accepting responsibility are necessary steps in living out the mission of the church today.

Analysis of Pope Francis's 2022 Apology

This dynamic of the "scandals of the past" as "an obstacle to the Church's witness today" is the operative dynamic in Pope Francis's apologies. A textual analysis of Pope Francis's apology in Maskwacis is helpful in assessing the apology. A close reading asks the questions "Does the pope apologize for himself, for the church, or for members of the church?" and "Does apology drive a distance between the church and the perpetrators?"

For example, Pope Benedict XVI once offered an apology to victims of sexual abuse by stating, "I am deeply sorry for the pain and suffering the victims have endured, and I assure them that, as their pastor, I too share in their suffering."[13] Pope Benedict XVI made no mention of the cover up of abuse or the role (or existence) of abusers; he spoke only of victims and their suffering, as though victims can exist without perpetrators. His identification with the victims may have been an attempt at solidarity, but I worry that it was instead a move away from recognizing his own role in clericalism and in protecting the hierarchy. The insistence that he, too, shared in the suffering of victims ran the risk of not recognizing the severity of the trauma that had resulted from the abuse. As a result, rather than being an act of solidarity, his apology can appear to have been out of touch.

Ecclesial apologies can be reminiscent of a "politician's apology," which utilizes the passive or conditional voice.[14] "Mistakes were made" – a passive sentence – may sound like an apology, but the lack of subject or actor obscures any sense of responsibility. Mistakes cannot be made abstractly; rather, a specific person makes mistakes. The passive voice fails to include the actor and, as a result, minimizes a sense of responsibility.

In looking at the language of responsibility in Pope Francis's apology, there are several aspects that stand out. First, as seen in the following passage, the pope apologized *a lot* in this apology statement:

> I have come to your native lands to tell you in person of my sorrow, to implore God's forgiveness, healing and reconciliation, to express my closeness and to pray with you and for you. I am here because the first step of my penitential pilgrimage among you is that of again asking forgiveness, of telling you once more that I am deeply sorry. Sorry for the ways in which, regrettably, many Christians supported the colonizing mentality of the powers that oppressed the indigenous peoples. I am sorry. I ask forgiveness, in particular, for the ways in which many members of the Church and of religious communities cooperated, not least through their indifference, in projects of cultural destruction and forced assimilation promoted by the governments of that time, which culminated in the system of residential schools.[15]

Pope Francis apologized for a wide range of actions by members of the church, along with their indifference and a colonizing mentality. This scope is an important dimension of the apology. I believe that it is a testament to the work done by Indigenous communities prior to the pope's visit, and recognition should go to the communities who engaged in this process.

Sometimes statements that we call apologies never actually contain the words "I'm sorry," or sometimes they defer responsibility. Notably, Pope Francis's apology in Maskwacis is different. The word "sorry" appears three times. Looking for synonyms is also instructive. "Forgiveness" appears five times and "beg/begging pardon" appears twice. "Church" appears only once, and "members of the Church" also appears once. "Healing" appears four times. Pope Francis does use "I" many times, and as the leader of the church, it is possible to interpret this as the royal "we," in which he speaks for the church. In my assessment, this language is indicative of a genuine intention to apologize and claim responsibility, albeit while still placing a slight distance between the church and the actions of the residential schools and rushing to a sense of healing. I am skeptical of the rush to healing, for it often places the responsibility on the victim to heal rather than on the perpetrator to render justice. Further, healing, especially in relation to trauma, does not proceed according to a linear time frame or occur within a specific timeline.

For all of his apologizing, Pope Francis still placed a distance between "the Church" and "members of the Church." This distance was also present in the pope's apology at the Vatican in April 2022, where he said, "For the deplorable conduct of these members of the Catholic Church, I ask for God's forgiveness, and I want to say to you with all my heart: I am very sorry."[16] We see Pope Francis say time and time again, "I am very sorry," which is an important advancement in papal apologies. However, he often points to "members of the Church," not the church itself, as the perpetrator.

For an apology to be credible and authentic, this distance must be bridged. As an ecclesiologist, I argue that the church must recognize the harm perpetrated in its name. Placing a distance fails to recognize the true harm and results in the apology ringing hollow. The word "church" can mean many different things, such as a building, the hierarchy, representatives of the church, priests, or the people of God. When the pope apologizes, he is positioned to do so in a way that speaks for the church as a whole. Rather than narrowing the definition of the church, the pope can and should be leaning into the multiple meanings of "church" to apologize for the multiple repercussions of harm. The harm perpetrated in the residential schools was carried out by individuals and institutions, and it is only fitting that the overarching institution– the Roman Catholic Church – take responsibility for the harm carried out in its name.

The closest that Pope Francis comes to accepting responsibility on behalf of the church itself is when he draws upon Pope John Paul II: "In the face of this deplorable evil, the Church kneels before God and implores his forgiveness for the sins of her children[17] ... I myself wish to reaffirm this, with shame and unambiguously. I humbly beg forgiveness for the evil committed by so many Christians against the indigenous peoples."[18] Noting that "the Church kneels before God" is a helpful step in taking responsibility, yet the phrase continues to ask forgiveness for "the sins of her children." Again, there is distance in this apology. This distance is characteristic of other papal apologies and leaves me wanting more accountability from the church.

Apologies and Action

A second notable area of this apology is the connection to actions before and after this papal visit. Apologies never happen in a vacuum, and Pope Francis explicitly connected his apology to prior actions, setting this apology apart from other papal apologies. For example, Pope Francis referenced the moccasins that he was asked to carry by the delegation visiting the Vatican four months prior:

> I recall the meetings we had in Rome four months ago. At that time, I was given two pairs of moccasins as a sign of the suffering endured by indigenous children, particularly those who, unfortunately, never came back from the residential schools. I was asked to return the moccasins when I came to Canada; I brought them, and I will return them at the end of these few words, in which I would like to reflect

> on this symbol, which over the past few months has kept alive my sense of sorrow, indignation and shame.[19]

Critics might say that there is no way to demonstrate whether this symbol or apology is genuine. It is true that there is no way to prove genuineness, and my goal here is not to argue one side or the other. Rather, I seek to point out what is unique about this apology compared to other apologies. The connection to these actions, driven by the Indigenous delegation that visited Rome earlier in the year,[20] is an intentional subversion of traditional power dynamics; Pope Francis continues to place himself in the role of penitential pilgrim and recognizes the agency of First Nations, Métis, and Inuit.

Further, Pope Francis recognizes that this apology is one step of many steps. This recognition is significant. Apologies are often perceived as the most important step, or even the only step, but the pope challenges this perception by placing his apology in a larger context. Regarding the apology as one step of many in a larger reconciliation process lends credence to its authenticity.

It is also significant that Pope Francis travelled to Indigenous lands to offer this apology, a request of the community. The importance of this aspect of the apology cannot be overstated. His presence acknowledged the connection of Indigenous Peoples to the land. At the same time, it attested to the divisive role of residential schools in the relationship to land, language, and culture. Importantly, the pope's visit to Canada at the request of Indigenous communities also affirmed that these communities have agency. The Truth and Reconciliation Commission of Canada, which administered a national process of truth telling, listening, and recognition of residential school survivors' experiences, outlined recommendations for future follow-up in its *Calls to Action* (2015). Call 58 states,

> We call upon the Pope to issue an apology to Survivors, their families, and communities for the Roman Catholic Church's role in the spiritual, cultural, emotional, physical, and sexual abuse of First Nations, Inuit, and Métis children in Catholic-run residential

> schools. We call for that apology to be similar to the 2010 apology issued to Irish victims of abuse and to occur within one year of the issuing of this Report and to be delivered by the Pope in Canada.[21]

This recommendation is an essential subversion of traditional power structures, where the pope's comfort, time, and power take precedence over the requests of others.

This is not the only time that Pope Francis travelled to a site of harm to apologize for sinful actions committed by the church. In 2015, he had travelled to Bolivia and apologized for the "grave sins" of colonization: "I humbly ask forgiveness, not only for the offense of the church herself, but also for crimes committed against the native peoples during the so-called conquest of America."[22] In this apology, Pope Francis speaks for the universal church, connecting the church of today to the church centuries ago when colonialism began. The symbolic role of visiting Indigenous land is also important, for it affirms the agency of those inviting others to their home. This agency is especially important in the context of residential schools, where agency was denied or minimized, with drastic measures taken in attempts to cut off Indigenous children from their culture, heritage, and land.

Above, I examine words of repentance that were common in the statement of apology in Maskwacis. Notably, there is another phrase in this apology related to actions that is worthy of analysis: "first step." Pope Francis says this phrase four times in his apology. He refers to this trip and apology as "the first step of my penitential pilgrimage" and as "this first step of my journey." Again, I think that this statement is a testament to the work done prior to the papal visit to Canada. Pope Francis even acknowledges this work: "Dear brothers and sisters, many of you and your representatives have stated that begging pardon is not the end of the matter. I fully agree: that is only the first step, the starting point."[23]

Traditionally, papal apologies were often presented as the final step, the culmination of the process, rather than as this initial step. Viewing an apology as the end of a process is a way of rushing the healing process or perhaps even completely ignoring the ongoing nature of healing. Healing is rarely complete, able to be checked off a to-do list and marked as final. Rather, the impact of trauma and harm can continue to unfold across a person's and community's life and experience, and as a result, healing continues as a nonlinear process. The role of apologies in a greater context of healing is acknowledged most clearly in the Truth and Reconciliation Commission's commentary on call 58: "Apologies mark only a beginning point on pathways of reconciliation; the proof of their authenticity lies in putting words into action."[24]

Papal apologies connect the past, present, and future. Flanagan argues that holy truth telling is essential for repentance: "Telling the truth about ecclesial error and about structural sinfulness is required out of fidelity to the memory of those who have been the victims of those errors. A starting point for repentance means taking seriously the pain of those, especially the relatively nameless or faceless ones, who have suffered because of the sinfulness of individual Christians, of individual leaders in the church and of the church community as a whole."[25] Pope Francis's apology recognizes the ongoing pain and suffering caused by the residential schools, as well as the memory of those who did not survive the residential school system. The pain knows no bounds. This apology is incredibly important, but it will fall flat if it is not connected with the larger context of culture, power, and abuse. To address this context, I now look at the repudiation of the Doctrine of Discovery.

AS THE CHURCH HAS ALWAYS TAUGHT: THE REPUDIATION OF THE DOCTRINE OF DISCOVERY

The 2023 repudiation of the Doctrine of Discovery illuminates this analysis of papal apologies.[26] The Doctrine of Discovery is a series of papal bulls or statements issued by the hierarchy of the Catholic Church that paved the way for colonialism in the fifteenth century, such as *Dum Diversas* (1452), *Romanus Pontifex* (1455), and *Inter Caetera* (1493). This teaching was written at a time when colonialism was changing the world landscape and perpetuating the misguided notion that Europeans brought

God to foreign lands. The Canadian Museum for Human Rights explains, "Both French and English colonial powers in what would later be known as Canada used the Doctrine of Discovery to claim Indigenous lands and force their cultural and religious beliefs on Indigenous peoples. Once Canada was created, the Doctrine of Discovery influenced the imposition of national, colonial laws on Indigenous peoples. This is because it denies the validity of long-standing systems of Indigenous governance and sovereignty."[27]

Overall, the repudiation of the Doctrine of Discovery has the potential to be a very helpful move forward for the church. Formally moving away from the Doctrine of Discovery impacts church teaching and seeps into theology and ecclesiology in many other ways. It can change the way that the church actualizes its experience of church. Saint Bede the Venerable is commonly noted for having said, "Every day the church gives birth to the church"; the repudiation of the Doctrine of Discovery changes the way that the church gives birth to the church. It paves the way for the church to live out a reality where it affirms the sanctity of all cultures, lands, and peoples. In a sense, it brings the church teaching of Vatican II on interreligious dialogue and ecumenism into alignment with other church teachings.

It is also important to note that many Indigenous Peoples called for the Catholic Church to rescind the Doctrine of Discovery during the papal visit in 2022.[28] We do not know the exact impact that these calls had on the repudiation, but the statement does cite "renewed dialogue with indigenous peoples" as a source of this change.[29] The statement continues,

> With their help, the Church has acquired a greater awareness of their sufferings, past and present, due to the expropriation of their lands, which they consider a sacred gift from God and their ancestors, as well as the policies of forced assimilation, promoted by the governmental authorities of the time, intended to eliminate their indigenous cultures.[30]

The repudiation of the Doctrine of Discovery could be understood as an instance of the further action indicated by Pope Francis, signalling that he was genuine in his calls for the apology to be the first of many steps.

The joint statement was issued by the Dicasteries for Culture and Education and for Promoting Integral Human Development. Although this statement is overall a positive step forward in actualizing a decolonial church in which the centres and peripheries are reordered and all cultures and peoples are valued, two aspects are troubling. First, the statement does not rescind the papal bulls on which the Doctrine of Discovery was based, including those noted above. The statement argues that "the 'doctrine of discovery' is not part of the teaching of the Catholic Church,"[31] a perplexing claim given that, to most people, it appeared to be a teaching. It is unclear how the Doctrine of Discovery is not to be considered part of church teaching given the high authoritative status of papal bulls. Perhaps the dicasteries mean to classify the Doctrine of Discovery as a practice of the church rather than a teaching of the church, although practical theology would resist such a division and instead affirm the connection of practice and teaching.

The statement continues, "Historical research clearly demonstrates that the papal documents in question, written in a specific historical period and linked to political questions, have never been considered expressions of the Catholic faith. At the same time, the Church acknowledges that these papal bulls did not adequately reflect the equal dignity and rights of indigenous peoples."[32] It is unclear to which historical research this statement is referring, and I question whether it is true that these bulls have "never been considered expressions of the Catholic faith," as such a statement seems difficult to assess. To be clear, it is good that this statement affirms that the teaching that undergirds the Doctrine of Discovery fails to recognize the dignity of all people and that the practice of colonialism is not grounded in authentic understandings of the Catholic faith. What is problematic is that this statement does not truly acknowledge the harm caused by these teachings and practices and does not speak to the need for restoration, reparation, and decolonial teaching and practice.

A textual analysis can provide insight into the deeper levels of a colonial mindset within this ecclesial document. I argue that the term "church" in the joint statement functions to create and promote a distance between the European church and Indigenous worldviews. I invite you critically to assess how the term "church" functions in this statement:

> In our own day, a renewed dialogue with indigenous peoples, especially with those who profess the Catholic Faith, has helped the Church to understand better their values and cultures ... The Church is committed to accompany indigenous peoples and to foster efforts aimed at promoting reconciliation and healing.[33]

It is in this context of listening to Indigenous Peoples that the church has heard the importance of addressing the concept referred to as the Doctrine of Discovery.[34] Who counts as "the Church" in the joint statement's repudiation of the Doctrine of Discovery? The term "church" is used in many different ways, including to refer to members of the church, to refer to the hierarchical church, and to express a sort of solidarity. As discussed at the beginning of this chapter, the term has a multiplicity of meanings. The many ways that "church" is employed in the joint statement illustrates the potentially problematic outcomes of stating "church" without contextualizing the term. Rather than enabling listeners to behold the mystery of the church, the lack of context can result in confusion.

The final paragraph of the joint statement continues, "More recently, the Church's solidarity with indigenous peoples has given rise to the Holy See's strong support for the principles contained in the United Nations Declaration on the Rights of Indigenous Peoples."[35] The words and actions here are important, but I am attentive to the way that the church frames itself as separate from Indigenous Peoples. It is analogous to the United States Conference of Catholic Bishops' pastoral letter on racism, entitled "Brothers and Sisters to Us" (1979).[36] Who is the *us*? Are African Americans and Black people not part of "us" in the church? In an effort at unity, there is a further division, a splitting of "us" from "them." There is also a normalizing of one group at the centre and a decentring of the other to the margins.

Likewise, are Indigenous Peoples not just members of the church but also part of the church? Who gets to claim the title of "church" and who are "members" or "brothers and sisters to us?" How the in-group and out-groups are determined reveals more about the power, privilege, and norming of the church than the document's words alone. There are no Indigenous and European churches; there is one church. The unity of the church is a tenet of Catholicism, yet the colonizing mentality can seep in, creating an "us" and a "them." However, the true mission of the church recognizes only a "we."

M. Shawn Copeland argues that the Enlightenment's "turn to the subject" was actually a turn to a specific subject: "white male bourgeois European being-in-the-world."[37] Copeland advances a move away from a "camouflage[d]" subject by "turning the subject."[38] Likewise, the operative ecclesiology of the hierarchical church would benefit from turning the subject. The subject of the church should not be a white male being who masquerades as neutral. Imagine how different Pope Francis's repudiation of the Doctrine of Discovery would be if the ecclesial subject was a survivor of residential schools.

If the spirit of the Doctrine of Discovery were truly repudiated, perhaps the sentiment that Indigenous Peoples are someone other than the church would not permeate the document. Until the church repudiates not just the teaching of the Doctrine of Discovery but also the underlying motivation to see some people as other, the church will continue to be characterized by a settler mentality.

CONTEXTUALIZATION AND RECEPTION OF APOLOGIES

Apologies are only one direction on the path of reconciliation. Forgiveness, healing, and reception, or lack thereof, are also important elements of this ecclesial act. Archbishop Donald Bolen of Regina, Saskatchewan, remarks, "Pope Francis's words of apology did not meet every request or expectation from survivors and Indigenous communities. For some, it did not say enough. For others, it brought healing. For still others, it was a step along the way, but one needing to be made real by being followed up with concrete actions, solidarity expressed in a way that builds relationships and restores trust."[39] As a white woman residing in the United States, it is not for me to speak for communities to whom the apology was directed. Instead, this ecclesiological analysis looks at the ways that reception may or may not happen.

A key foundation for the possibility of reception of an apology and reconciliation is the genuineness of the apology. Judith Herman, a trauma studies scholar, explores the need for apologies to be genuine or risk doing further harm. Based on her work with trauma survivors on healing, she concludes, "While genuine apologies foster the hope that evil deeds can be redeemed, insincere apologies add insult to injury by mocking that hope."[40] Ecclesial apologies risk being insincere and, in the words of Herman, mocking hope. The mission of the church is to deepen and strengthen hope, not to undercut it.

Apologies can be insincere when they appear to be a "politician's apology,"[41] spoken in the passive voice and failing to take responsibility. Parts one and two of this chapter look at how creating a distance, including distance from the perpetrator as well as distance from the victims, led to a lack of responsibility. Another factor that can result in an insincere apology is pressure on those to whom the apology is directed to rush to forgiveness. Herman notes how this dynamic affects victims-survivors: "To the extent that they felt social pressure toward forgiveness, they tended to resent and resist it."[42] In an ecclesial setting, the pressure to forgive can be exacerbated by the power differential between a priest or church leader and the laity, particularly when the laity includes Indigenous people. Further, the intense media attention to Pope Francis's trip to Canada may have contributed to a pressure to rush to forgiveness. Within hours of Pope Francis's apology, there was discussion in the media about whether the apology was genuine and whether the communities to whom it was addressed would receive the apology.[43] Such a rush to the outcome can undermine the apology process.

More than anything, a genuine apology hinges on the hope that the future will be different. Herman explains, "True apology also offers a promise, implicit or explicit, that the offender has undergone a moral awakening: that he is a changed man and will never repeat his crime."[44] To offer an apology with no hope of change is not to apologize. Likewise, apologies that are not grounded in an understanding of the immorality of the originating act(s) are insincere and mock hope. This "moral awakening" can look different in differing circumstances and can be difficult to assess, but it can be lived out in the actions that follow.

For the papal apology to ring true – for the church to transform – the church and theological endeavour must engage in a process of decolonization. This undertaking involves efforts of the hierarchy, but it is also a call for a greater ecclesial shift. Debora Tonelli describes decolonial theology as requiring "the readiness to dialogue of both former colonized and colonizers at a high-quality level,"[45] yet this dialogue is not the only aspect of decolonial theology. Tonelli continues, "The issue at stake is not only the reconciliation with the past but the building of new identities and a new global order, and this can only be an ongoing process."[46] As with the repudiation of the Doctrine of Discovery, it is not enough simply to reject the past. Instead, the entire church must engage in a process of unraveling the ways that it is infused by the settler-colonial enterprise.

The church cannot engage in decolonization if the Doctrine of Discovery is still in place, yet the move away from this doctrine is not enough to bring about reconciliation. It may be part of the "moral awakening" necessary for apologizing and starting the process of reconciliation, but it is not sufficient. The repudiation of the Doctrine of Discovery is a step, but it is not a complete journey.

The word "tradition" is rooted in the Latin word *tradere* (to hand on). Unity and justice can be passed along from generation to generation, or trauma and harm can be passed along. With the papacy of Pope Leo XIV, it will be interesting to see how Pope Francis's legacy of apologizing is passed along. Will Pope Leo bridge the distance between the church as victim and perpetrator? Will local bishops' groups engage in restorative practices with communities that have been harmed by the church? There is great potential for the church to fulfill its mission of spreading the good news of the Gospel if it heeds the call to repentance, repair, restoration, and working for justice. My hope is that all of the church, including the faithful, will embody this call.

NOTES

The author thanks members of the Canadian Theological Society for helpful discussions about early versions of this chapter and Katie Kolodziej for her thoughtful read of its later development.

1 Examples include Chico Harlan and Amanda Coletta, "Pope Apologizes for 'Evil Committed by so Many Christians' in Canada's Residential Schools," *Washington Post*, 26 July 2022, https://www.washingtonpost.com/world/2022/07/25/pope-francis-apology-canada-residential-homes/; Nicole Winfield and Peter Smith, "Pope Apologizes for 'Catastrophic' School Policy in Canada," Associated Press, 26 July 2022, https://apnews.com/article/pope-francis-canada-apology-visit-137ad23719603e9d370257f257ec0163; Associated Press, "Pope Francis Issues an Historic Apology for 'Devastating' School Abuses in Canada," NPR, 25 July 2022, https://www.npr.org/2022/07/25/1113378991/pope-apology-canada-indigenous-schools.

2 Pope Francis, "Angelus," 17 July 2022, https://www.vatican.va/content/francesco/en/angelus/2022/documents/20220717-angelus.html.

3 Pope Francis, "Address of His Holiness: Maskwacis," 25 July 2022, https://www.vatican.va/content/francesco/en/speeches/2022/july/documents/20220725-popolazioniindigene-canada.html.

4 Holy See Press Office, "Joint Statement of the Dicasteries for Culture and Education and for Promoting Integral Human Development on the 'Doctrine of Discovery,'" 30 March 2023, https://press.vatican.va/content/salastampa/it/bollettino/pubblico/2023/03/30/0238/00515.html.

5 Georgetown University, "Georgetown Reflects on Slavery, Memory, and Reconciliation," n.d., https://www.georgetown.edu/slavery/; Rachel L. Swarns, *The 272: The Families Who Were Enslaved and Sold to Build the American Catholic Church* (New York: Random House, 2023).

6 Pope Adrian VI had a short tenure as pope: twenty-months from 1522 to 1523. Luigi Accattoli, *When a Pope Asks Forgiveness: The Mea Culpas of John Paul II* (Boston: Pauline Books and Media, 1998), 5.

7 Accattoli, *When a Pope Asks*, 8.

8 The Pastoral Constitution puts forth a vision of the church in the modern world as part of the world rather than separated from it: "Though mankind is stricken with wonder at its own discoveries and its power, it often raises anxious questions about the current trend of the world, about the place and role of man in the universe, about the meaning of its individual and collective strivings, and about the ultimate destiny of reality and of humanity. Hence, giving witness and voice to the faith of the whole people of God gathered together by Christ, this council can provide no more eloquent proof of its solidarity with, as well as its respect and love for the entire human family with which it is bound up, than by engaging with it in conversation about these various problems. The council brings to mankind light kindled from the Gospel, and puts at its disposal those saving resources which the Church herself, under the guidance of the Holy Spirit, receives from her Founder. For the human person deserves to be preserved; human society deserves to be renewed. Hence the focal point of our total presentation will be man himself, whole and entire, body and soul, heart and conscience, mind and will." Second Vatican Council, *Gaudium et Spes* (1965), para. 3, http://www.vatican.va/archive/hist_councils/ii_vatican_council/documents/vat-ii_const_19651207_gaudium-et-spes_en.html.

9 Brian P. Flanagan, *Stumbling in Holiness: Sin and Sanctity in the Church* (Collegeville, MN: Liturgical Press Academic, 2018), 104–5.

10 See section headings in Second Vatican Council, *Lumen Gentium* (1964), http://www.vatican.va/archive/hist_councils/ii_vatican_council/documents/vat-ii_const_19641121_lumen-gentium_en.html.

11 Jeremy M. Bergen, *Ecclesial Repentance: The Churches Confront Their Sinful Pasts* (London: T&T Clark, 2011), 269.

12 International Theological Commission, *Memory and Reconciliation: The Church and the Faults of the Past* (1999), sec. 1.4, https://www.vatican.va/roman_curia/congregations/cfaith/cti_documents/rc_con_cfaith_doc_20000307_memory-reconc-itc_en.html.

13 Quoted in Barney Zwartz, "Pope Sorry for 'Pain and Suffering,'" *Sydney Morning Herald*, 20 July 2008, https://www.smh.com.au/national/pope-sorry-for-pain-and-suffering-20080719-3hy1.html.

14 Judith L. Herman, *Truth and Repair: How Trauma Survivors Envision Justice* (New York: Basic Books, 2023), 99.
15 Pope Francis, "Address of His Holiness: Maskwacis."
16 "Read Pope Francis's Full Remarks, Apology for Abuses by Some Catholic Church Members in Residential Schools," CBC *News*, 1 April 2022, https://www.cbc.ca/news/world/francis-apology-full-text-1.6404953.
17 Here, the address cites Pope John Paul II, *Incarnationis Mysterium* (1998), no. 11, https://www.vatican.va/jubilee_2000/docs/documents/hf_jp-ii_doc_30111998_bolla-jubilee_en.html.
18 Pope Francis, "Address of His Holiness: Maskwacis."
19 Pope Francis, "Address of His Holiness: Maskwacis."
20 For more information on the delegation to Rome, see Catholic Archdiocese of Edmonton, "Delegation To Rome – 2022," n.d., https://caedm.ca/offices/indigenous-relations/indigenous-delegation-to-rome-2022/.
21 Truth and Reconciliation Commission of Canada, *Calls to Action* (2015), no. 58, https://www2.gov.bc.ca/assets/gov/british-columbians-our-governments/indigenous-people/aboriginal-peoples-documents/calls_to_action_english2.pdf.
22 Quoted in Jim Yardley and William Neuman, "In Bolivia, Pope Francis Apologizes for Church's 'Grave Sins,'" *New York Times*, 10 July 2015, https://www.nytimes.com/2015/07/10/world/americas/pope-francis-bolivia-catholic-church-apology.html.
23 Pope Francis, "Address of His Holiness: Maskwacis."
24 Truth and Reconciliation Commission of Canada, *Honouring the Truth, Reconciling for the Future: Summary of the Final Report of the Truth and Reconciliation Commission of Canada* (2015), 224, https://ehprnh2mwo3.exactdn.com/wp-content/uploads/2021/01/Executive_Summary_English_Web.pdf.
25 Flanagan, *Stumbling in Holiness*, 106.
26 Holy See Press Office, "Joint Statement of the Dicasteries."
27 Travis Tomchuk, "The Doctrine of Discovery," Canadian Museum for Human Rights, 11 May 2023, https://humanrights.ca/story/doctrine-discovery.
28 In the Truth and Reconciliation Commission's *Calls to Action* (2015), re-

pudiation of the Doctrine of Discovery is listed as action items directed both at governments and at religious institutions. Call 47 reads, "We call upon federal, provincial, territorial, and municipal governments to repudiate concepts used to justify European sovereignty over Indigenous Peoples and lands, such as the Doctrine of Discovery and terra nullius, and to reform those laws, government policies, and litigation strategies that continue to rely on such concepts." And call 49 states, "We call upon all religious denominations and faith groups who have not already done so to repudiate concepts used to justify European sovereignty over Indigenous lands and peoples, such as the Doctrine of Discovery and *terra nullius*."

29 Holy See Press Office, "Joint Statement of the Dicasteries," para. 4.

30 Holy See Press Office, "Joint Statement of the Dicasteries," para. 4.

31 Holy See Press Office, "Joint Statement of the Dicasteries," para. 6.

32 Holy See Press Office, "Joint Statement of the Dicasteries," para. 6.

33 Holy See Press Office, "Joint Statement of the Dicasteries," para. 4.

34 Holy See Press Office, "Joint Statement of the Dicasteries," para. 5.

35 Holy See Press Office, "Joint Statement of the Dicasteries," para. 9.

36 United States Conference of Catholic Bishops, "Brothers and Sisters to Us: U.S. Catholic Bishops Pastoral Letter on Racism," 1979, https://www.usccb.org/committees/african-american-affairs/brothers-and-sisters-us.

37 M. Shawn Copeland, *Enfleshing Freedom: Body, Race, and Being*, 2nd ed. (Minneapolis, MN: Fortress Press, 2023), 78.

38 Copeland, *Enfleshing Freedom*, 91.

39 Donald Bolen, "The Papal Apology and Seeds of an Action Plan," *Journal of Moral Theology* 12, no. 1 (2023): 46, https://jmt.scholasticahq.com/article/66234-the-papal-apology-and-seeds-of-an-action-plan.

40 Herman, *Truth and Repair*, 98.

41 Herman, *Truth and Repair*, 105.

42 Herman, *Truth and Repair*, 105.

43 For example, within hours, the Associated Press published a story titled "Pope Francis Issues an Historic Apology for 'Devastating' School Abuses in Canada." This news article and the others cited in note 1 were all published within twenty-four hours of the apology.

44 Herman, *Truth and Repair*, 93.

45 Debora Tonelli, "Decolonial Theology and Changing the Global Church," *Berkley Forum*, blog, 23 September 2020, https://berkleycenter.georgetown.edu/responses/decolonial-theology-and-changing-the-global-church.

46 Tonelli, "Decolonial Theology."

4

Delocality and Colonial Apologies
A Critical Assessment of the Papal Apologies at Maskwacis and Lac Ste Anne

Timothy Harvie

In 2015, the Truth and Reconciliation Commission of Canada (TRC) published the initial summary of its findings and its *Calls to Action* in seeking justice from both the Canadian government and the various religious bodies responsible for the horrors of the residential school system.[1] Of these calls, the fifty-eighth summoned the pope to issue an apology on traditional lands in what is now Canada. Despite there being precedence for such an act – indeed, the calls cite the 2010 papal apology to survivors of the abuse scandal in Ireland[2] – seven years would pass before Pope Francis heeded the appeal of Indigenous leaders to come to Canada and offer a public apology. As a settler Canadian located in the Roman Catholic tradition and living in Treaty 7 territory, I reflect critically here on a couple of moments in Alberta during what Pope Francis called his "penitential pilgrimage" to Canada:[3] his apology at Maskwacis and the speech at Lac Ste Anne. My discussion of these events is an attempt to listen to Indigenous scholarship and to the testimonies and conclusions of the Truth and Reconciliation Commission in dialogue with my own work in eco-public theology.

LAND

The apology at Maskwacis was a first step in a journey of contrition and reconciliation that will take generations. In his apology, Pope Francis located himself in the territories of Indigenous Peoples, whose relationship to the land and its myriad inhabitants is intergenerational and from time immemorial.[4] He recognized the colonization enacted by European settlers and, in his engagement with the media on the plane back to Rome, acknowledged openly the genocide that had taken place in Canada.[5] Much of the apology focused on the roles that Catholic bodies and organizations played in the abuse and devastation wrought by the residential schools. I do not deliberate here on the merits of public apologies per se or on the church's eschewal of institutional sin in favour of the repeated statements that sins were committed by individual "members of the Church" rather than by the church itself. Nor do I focus on the Vatican's more formal disavowal of the Doctrine of Discovery,[6] which limits the scope of culpability in saying that "many Christians" took part in these abominable acts but not the institution of the church itself.[7] Rather, I focus my reflections on the apologies themselves and on how they exhibit a tension between locating oneself either within the particularity of land and its constitutive formation of communities and spiritualities or within the totalizing and universalizing tendencies found in colonial practices of dislocation.

At Maskwacis, Pope Francis noted the role of pilgrimage to this particular land. He said, "These lands speak to us; they enable us to remember."[8] The recognition of how we are tied to land is central in this opening statement and acknowledges an essential feature of his pilgrimage. The theme of pilgrimage has developed a widespread literature that stretches across disciplines in theology, ethnography, anthropology, and sociology, among others. Within these discussions, there are two essential themes. Anthropologists Victor Turner and Edith Turner have noted the role of "communitas" in pilgrimage.[9] Here, the shared experience of diverse peoples coming together for a shared ritual with a common heritage of symbols and traditions works to unite individuals in the community of shared experience. Anthropologists John Eade and Michael J. Sallnow dispute the overarching theme of communitas in their argument that pilgrimage sites are contested spaces where competing views, experiences, and participation offer a disjunctive experience between the pilgrims.[10] Any attempt to understand the role and function of pilgrimage must include both historical and personal narratives alongside primary and secondary research.[11] Relevant to the journey of Pope Francis is what Orthodox theologian Dragos Herescu has called the "metanoic" aspect of pilgrimage.[12] The necessity of life change both for the individual and for the community expresses the transformational aspect of pilgrimage, which aims to achieve spiritual repentance, renewal, and conversion. With this transformational component, Herescu offers a caution that could also be made to the Canadian bishops in the wake of Pope Francis's penitential pilgrimage: pilgrimages are not "quick-fix opportunities" or "panacea events" but are "integral parts of a life-long process of change."[13]

Both community and contestation are present in the penitential pilgrimage, as illuminated through the lens of the land. Pope Francis recognized at Maskwacis that Indigenous Peoples have lived with the land in that particular location since "time immemorial" and that from the land comes "a treasury of sound customs and teachings."[14] This statement echoes the insight that Pope Francis had expressed in his encyclical *Laudato Si'* (2015), where he discerns that Indigenous Peoples "are not merely one minority among others, but should be the principal dialogue partners, especially when large projects affecting their land are proposed."[15] However, in Canada, land has been a contested place, particularly due to the domination over land exercised by colonial powers and their failure to recognize that Indigenous governments have a deep connection to land. As Angele Alook and colleagues have noted, "Indigenous people did not believe one could own the land; therefore, the sale of land did not make sense. To Indigenous people, Treaties were regarded as land-use frameworks and agreements for sharing the land in mutual coexistence."[16] It is precisely where disputes over land emerge that much of the ongoing colonial impact is seen, an outcome that is especially common with land treatment in an age of climate crisis. Just as the divine mandate of the church was used to justify its mission in what is now Canada, including its support for the policies of the Canadian government's residential schools, the profit of business is used today to justify the marginalization and silencing of Indigenous land claims. "Because settler governments assume the land to be theirs until proven otherwise," Alook and colleagues write, "Canadian courts deem activities that impede business to be illegal."[17]

In *Pollution Is Colonialism* (2021), which discusses the connection between colonialism and land, Métis scholar Max Liboiron writes, "Assumed access by settler and colonial projects to Indigenous lands for settler and colonial goals" is an essential feature of Western industry and science and is indicative of settler relations.[18] Here, even efforts at environmental conservation exhibit an "assumed entitlement" and access to Indigenous lands.[19] Indeed, Liboiron concludes that "colonialism, first, foremost, and always, is about Land."[20]

This insight echoes findings reported in the sixth volume of the TRC's final report, where Anishinaabe elder Fred Kelly is quoted as saying, "To take the territorial lands away from a people whose very spirit is so intrinsically connected to Mother Earth was to actually dispossess them of their very soul and being; it was to destroy whole Indigenous nations."[21] Similarly, Mi'kmaq elder Stephen Augustine "suggested that … our relationships with the earth and all living beings are also relevant in working towards reconciliation."[22] The report offers an indictment of settler-land relations when it states, "If human beings resolve problems between themselves but continue to destroy the natural world, then reconciliation remains incomplete."[23] In calling attention to the land, Pope Francis not only highlighted the deep histories that the Treaty 6 Cree, Dene, Saulteaux, Nakota Sioux, and Métis nations have with the land and its nonhuman inhabitants but also acknowledged the ways that relationships with the land have been fractured by the violence of colonialism and by the instrumentalizing approach that colonial industries take in their dealings with the earth.

Even more than his predecessors, Pope Francis devoted much discussion both to the ill-treatment of the earth and to the climate crisis. In his encyclical *Laudato Si'* the pope repeatedly draws attention to the land. He cites sabbatical laws allowing the land to rest, describes the abundance of the land for both human and nonhuman inhabitants, and continually describes how the earth itself offers praise.[24] In doing so, he laments the technocratic paradigm, which views the earth and its inhabitants as mere instruments of capital, resulting in what he calls a throwaway culture.[25] In this culture, all living things and the earth itself are ultimately disposable and without intrinsic dignity of their own. In his apostolic exhortation of 2023, *Laudate Deum*, Pope Francis addresses these themes once more, although with a sharper edge. Here, he criticizes more directly the technocratic paradigm, which holds that "nonhuman reality is a mere resource at [human] disposal."[26] Again, Pope Francis addresses the model set forward by Indigenous Peoples' own relationship to the land. He writes, "A healthy ecology is also the result of interaction between humans and the environment, as occurs in the indigenous cultures and has occurred for centuries in different regions of the earth."[27]

Despite these positive advances, Pope Francis – along with the Catholic tradition as a whole – still struggled to reconfigure its largely anthropocentric and, indeed, Western standpoint. Francis recognized the inherent dignity of the more-than-human world, but maintained that it could still be instrumentalized, albeit within a more limited scope.[28] In *Laudate Deum*, he acknowledges that "human beings must be recognized as a part of nature."[29] However, he fails to come to terms with the unique agency of land, its role as life-giver and teacher, and so does not do justice to the particular spiritual, material, generational, and relational connections to the land found in the Indigenous cultures that he addressed on his penitential pilgrimage.[30] This failure is typified by the alleged universalism claimed by Western thought, which removes particularity and locality from its pronouncements in favour of claims to hold an external, hierarchical, and objective viewpoint. A failure to recognize the locality of our own earthen embeddedness came to the fore even as Pope Francis addressed the Indigenous Peoples in Canada. Here, his aim to reorient Catholics and the world to reconsider the place of the earth and its lands stood in tension with the abstraction of this aim from any locality itself.

This tension can be seen in his address at Lac Ste Anne, where he acknowledges the role of land in the lives of Indigenous people but is able to do so only in a limited way that ends up moving the focus of the audience away from the land that they are on and toward a universalizing, and thus colonizing, account conceptualized without the particularity of their location.[31]

DELOCALITY

Although the pope's meditations at Lac Ste Anne began with the sound of drums and despite the nearness of the water to where he stood, it quickly became clear that his thoughts did not attend to this location. Rather, Lac Ste Anne and the traditional lands on which he stood merely served as a reminder of the biblical locations of Galilee and as an invocation of the gospel texts of the New Testament that recount the related narratives. Even more so, the actual waters of Galilee became useful only as illustrations of the metaphorical waters seen flowing from the temple in the vision of the Hebrew prophet Ezekiel.[32] In this way, Pope Francis removed his audience from the lands on which they stood in order to appropriate the image for another, universalizing portrayal – that of Galilee and the Christian story. This is an example of what American Cherokee philosopher Brian Burkhart refers to as "delocality."[33] Delocality is the colonial claim to universality that does not speak from a particular location but sees itself as making claims to all locations. Rather than speaking from Lac Ste Anne, Pope Francis presumed to speak over Lac Ste Anne from Galilee and, even then, not as one rooted in the Galilean landscape but as one making a literary and theological allusion. This positioning contrasts with locality, which, according to Burkhart, "is being-from-the-land and knowing-from-the-land."[34] For Burkhart, the relationship between locality and delocality is both an epistemic and a metaphysical reality. The divergence between the two is where colonialism obscures and seeks to erase the particularity of relations that are rooted in the concrete specificity of place. Burkhart suggests that "from the spatial point of view, the actual land and the particularity of that actual land matter much and function formatively and continually in the moral, epistemological, historical, and religious life of a people."[35]

In the Western mindset, the transposition of land into an abstractable concept is rooted in the Lockean notion of property. For Burkhart, the starting place in this notion is those human beings (indeed, European males) who dominate land through work, thus making it an inviolable possession.[36] In the colonial history of Canada, this mixing of one's labour with land neglected the ways that Indigenous cultures had worked with the land since time immemorial. Colonialism was less about uncovering a possible means to understand the relationship of humans to land and more about the justification of subjugation of both earth and peoples to the colonial will. For Locke, Indigenous Peoples were living in a co-called state of nature, thus justifying English colonial practices.

According to Locke's account of this so-called state of nature, humans were entirely self-possessed and thus had inalienable rights, which justified their use of land.[37] However, in Locke's writings, it is clear that use of land and right to property are contingent on European modes of enclosure, agriculture, and labour.[38] Thus, although Locke holds that in a state of nature Indigenous persons may make use of the natural fruits of the land, he determines that this use does not constitute ownership through the demarcation of particular portions as separate from the commons because this demarcation requires European tilling and farming. Indeed, Locke holds that agreements, covenants, and contracts between Europeans and Indigenous people who remain in the state of nature are not binding in terms of propertied land being recognized as owned through labour.[39] In redefining what constituted the people, land, and power, Western colonial authorities saw fit to displace Indigenous persons from the land. According to Burkhart, this was so much the case that "redefinition is in fact the key to understanding the settler logic of Locke's definition of property."[40] In contrast to the Lockean perspective, Indigenous frameworks seek embodied relationship with the land and its inhabitants, with whom all have a familial relation. Land is material and embodied and therefore relational and local.[41]

In his ruminations at Lac Ste Anne, Pope Francis recognized the enculturation of Catholic faith in referencing Our Lady of Guadalupe. Although this incarnation of the Virgin Mary appeared to Christian convert Juan Diego in 1531, speaking his Nahuatl language and dressed in traditional attire, the pope claimed that she brought "the true faith to the indigenous people."[42] He proceeded to praise the missionaries and evangelizers who communicated the Christian faith but failed to recognize that disentangling the colonizing educations and community ruptures is not easily accomplished through such evangelizing. Indeed, the emphases struck at Lac Ste Anne exhibited what the director of research for the TRC, Paulette Regan, identifies as the tendency of apologies to "reinforce the colonial status quo."[43] The delocality in Pope Francis's approach to land allowed him to perpetuate a universalizing claim for Christian faith in opposition to the traditional spiritual and religious practices of the nations of Treaty 6, which arise from relations with the land.

Métis scholar Sharon Jarvis highlights this delocality in an imaginative dialogue between herself, Pope Francis, and indigenous scholar Michael Marker. Jarvis highlights the distinction between the Western concept of land ownership and the Indigenous view of "sharing and caring with and for the land."[44] Throughout the hypothetical discussion, Jarvis continually seeks to reorient the settler mindset away from land as object or land as property in order to highlight the spiritual connection of Indigenous communities to the land in a familial relationship. In centring the relationship to land, it is clear that a community of the land is required "to reteach the culture of care and share" and that there is a "metaphysical imperative" to understand locality and learn to live from the land.[45] In removing attention from the land in his Lac Ste Anne homily, Pope Francis failed to listen adequately to what he might have learned from the stories arising from the locality of a specific place. Instead, the delocalizing tendencies typified in colonial relationships remained the driving narrative feature of the address.

An issue arising from this reality is that Pope Francis set himself up, and indeed the Catholic Church in Canada as a whole, as teacher and leader in this discussion. He highlighted how Our Lady of Guadalupe, and himself as a representative of her message, had come to bring the true faith to a people lacking its fullness. He decentred the particular in favour of the universal and displaced the land on which he stood in preference for biblical and metaphorical lands. The cumulative effect was a reinforcement of the hierarchical and colonial relationships that had been the cause of his pilgrimage in the first place. Although he was deeply aware of the reality of human suffering and had listened closely to the stories of the victims of the church in a genuine encounter,[46] he recapitulated not only the intellectual and relational habits of removal but also the totalizing placement of the particular into universal, and therefore abstract, categories. In doing so, he exhibited the delocality illuminated and critiqued by Burkhart without the recognition of his own limiting framework. By emphasizing the bringing of the true faith to Indigenous persons, the speech at Lac Ste Anne prepared the way for Catholic evangelization to proceed. However, what Pope Francis neglected to note was that on these lands, it is the church in Canada that needs to be evangelized and taught how to live well with its fellow creatures and the land itself. Just as the church is called to ecological conversion in *Laudato Si'* (2015), the Church in Canada needs to be converted to a new relationship with the territories in which it stands. It needs to learn how to divest itself of a proprietary relationship to the land and enter into a relationship of caring and sharing where the lands and its Indigenous Peoples are teachers.

PENITENCE

With regard once more to the testimonies of the TRC, Pope Francis and the Catholic Church in Canada would do well to heed the comments of honorary witness Wab Kinew, who admonished, "The truth about reconciliation is this: it is not a second chance at assimilation. It should not be a kinder, gentler evangelism."[47] Indeed, we settler Canadians who are Catholic ought to take seriously the recommendation of elder Jim Dumont, who testified, "But what bothers me about it is that the church continues to have a hold on our people … Just get out of the way for awhile so that we can do what we need to do because as long as you are standing there thinking that you are supporting us, you are actually preventing us from getting to our own truth about this and our own healing."[48] The church must be converted to a new relationship with the earth in concrete and particular ways rather than holding to the delocalizing and universalizing ways present even in Pope Francis's penitential pilgrimage. The church can no longer presume to be teachers. We must become humble, quiet, and listening students of the particular lands in which we are treaty partners. We must wait for an invitation from Indigenous Peoples to become their students. We must repent of how we have spiritually isolated our institution from the realities of ecclesial and structural sin. We must repent of claims to religious superiority and of being possessors of *the* truth, as though we are adequate in our spiritual seclusion – as though we alone are sufficient.

A genuine repentance comes from the metanoic aspect of pilgrimage and cannot be encapsulated in the visit of a single individual, even one such as Pope Francis. There is no panacea in the journey of reconciliation. The posture of repentance envisioned here requires the Catholic Church in Canada to make reconciliation a central part of the spiritual development of each diocese, bishop, priest, parish, and person. Repentance will be visible in an abdication of the presumption to speak authoritatively on what it means to live in communion on and with these lands. It will recognize that many of our spiritual and ecological ills are due to the fact that, in adopting a proprietary relationship to the land as though settler Canadians "discovered" this place, we fail to comprehend the meaning of relationship with our fellow humans, our fellow creatures, and the Creator. Repentance will acknowledge that our spiritual infancy in the Canadian Catholic Church perpetuates systems of violence and the occlusion of the wisdom of Indigenous elders and knowledge keepers about land relations.

The penitential practice of humility requires a lifelong posture that seeks to listen and learn. A humble church will not impose its voice or its teaching but will recognize its own need to learn in an ongoing, intergenerational effort to reflect on the ways that the core assumptions at the bedrock of settler society and spirituality are in desperate need of alteration. To embody this effort, Pope Francis's apologies must be recognized not as the final word but as merely the first, incomplete gesture toward the healing of a relationship that cannot be placed on a timeline set by settler Canadians. Bishops and settler Catholics need to "get out of the way for awhile," and if invited to return, they must do so as postulants and neophytes needing the guidance of elders and knowledge keepers.

CONCLUSION

The penitential pilgrimage of Pope Francis was a necessary step in reconciliation. It was expressed in the TRC's *Calls to Action* (2015) as an essential part of the process in healing the colonial relations of Canada and the Catholic Church with Indigenous nations. However beneficial pilgrimages may be, they are only a potential means to a lifelong metanoic process. Pope Francis's addresses exhibit both the possibilities of community and the realities of context that shaped his apologies and his understandings of the Catholic Church's harmful and colonial activities. Notably, they demonstrate the delocalizing tendencies in Western thought and reify universalizing and totalizing claims with an evangelistic tone of bringing *the* truth, which can be gleaned only from Christianity's teachings. In doing so, his apologies display the ongoing necessity of the Catholic Church in Canada to expose and criticize how its own colonizing assumptions continue to operationalize its relationship to Indigenous Peoples. Although Pope Francis was attuned to the suffering of peoples and sought genuine encounter, he still adopted an approach that occluded the unique land relations expressed in Burkhart's account of locality. Thus the Catholic Church in Canada has much more work to do toward reconciliation. However, the church cannot maintain its supposed position as teacher and evangelizer. It must step aside, humble itself, and adopt the posture of the penitent and the student in dire need of the wisdom of elders and knowledge keepers.

NOTES

1 Truth and Reconciliation Commission of Canada (TRC), *Calls to Action* (2015), https://www2.gov.bc.ca/assets/gov/british-columbians-our-governments/indigenous-people/aboriginal-peoples-documents/calls_to_action_english2.pdf.

2 TRC, *Calls to Action*, no. 58.

3 Pope Francis, "Angelus," 17 July 2022, https://www.vatican.va/content/francesco/en/angelus/2022/documents/20220717-angelus.html.

4 Pope Francis, "Address of His Holiness: Maskwacis," 25 July 2022, https://www.vatican.va/content/francesco/en/speeches/2022/july/documents/20220725-popolazioniindigene-canada.html.

5 Pope Francis stated, "I didn't use it because it didn't come to my mind. But I described it as true, yes, it was genocide, yes, yes, no problem. You go ahead and say that I said yes, it was genocide. Thank you." Pope Francis, "Press Conference on the Return Flight to Rome," 29 July 2022, https://www.vatican.va/content/francesco/en/speeches/2022/july/documents/20220729-voloritorno-canada.html.

6 Holy See Press Office, "Joint Statement of the Dicasteries for Culture and Education and for Promoting Integral Human Development on the 'Doctrine of Discovery,'" 30 March 2023, https://press.vatican.va/content/salastampa/en/bollettino/pubblico/2023/03/30/230330b.html.

7 For more on this eschewal, see Jeremy M. Bergen, "Papal Apologies for Residential Schools and the Stories They Tell," *Journal of Moral Theology* 12, no. 1 (2023): 48–62.

8 Pope Francis, "Address of His Holiness: Maskwacis."

9 Victor Turner and Edith Turner, *Image and Pilgrimage in Christian Culture* (New York: Columbia University Press, 1978).

10 John Eade and Michael J. Sallnow, eds, *Contesting the Sacred: The Anthropology of Christian Pilgrimage* (1991; reprint, New York: Routledge, 2000).

11 Judith King, "The Struggle to Define Pilgrimage," *Religions* 14, no. 1 (2023): 1–11.

12 Dragos Herescu, "Seeking the Sacred through Pilgrimage: A Theological Perspective," *Journal of Orthodox Christian Studies* 4, no. 1 (2021): 23.

13 Herescu, "Seeking the Sacred," 24.

14 Pope Francis, "Address of His Holiness: Maskwacis."

15 Pope Francis, *Laudato Si'*, 24 May 2015, par. 146, https://www.vatican.va/content/francesco/es/encyclicals/documents/papa-francesco_20150524_enciclica-laudato-si.html.

16 Angele Alook, Emily Eaton, David Gray-Donald, Joël *LaForest, Crystal Lameman, and Bronwen Tucker, The End of This World: Climate Justice in So-Called Canada (Toronto: Between the Lines, 2023), 25.*

17 Alook et al., *End of This World*, 46.

18 Max Liboiron, *Pollution Is Colonialism* (Durham, NC: Duke University Press, 2021), 5.

19 Liboiron, *Pollution Is Colonialism*, 9.

20 Liboiron, *Pollution Is Colonialism*, 10.

21 TRC, *The Final Report of the Truth and Reconciliation Commission of Canada*, vol. 6, *Canada's Residential Schools: Reconciliation* (Montreal and Kingston: McGill-Queen's University Press, 2015), 103, https://publications.gc.ca/site/eng/9.807830/publication.html.

22 TRC, *Final Report*, vol. 6, 13.

23 TRC, *Final Report*, vol. 6, 13.

24 Pope Francis, *Laudato Si'*, par. 11.

25 Pope Francis, *Laudato Si'*, pars 20–2.

26 Pope Francis, *Laudate Deum*, 4 October 2023, par. 22, https://www.vatican.va/content/francesco/en/apost_exhortations/documents/20231004-laudate-deum.html.

27 Pope Francis, *Laudate Deum*, par. 27.

28 Pope Francis, *Laudato Si'*, pars 25, 130–6. See also *Catechism of the Catholic Church* (1992), part 1, sec. 1, ch. 2, art. 3, par. 130, https://www.vatican.va/archive/ENG0015/_INDEX.HTM#fonte.

29 Pope Francis, *Laudate Deum*, par. 26.

30 Matthew Eaton and I have written on the complicated and at times ambivalent approach to the more-than-human world in Catholicism and particularly in *Laudato Si'*. See Matthew Eaton and Timothy Harvie, "Laudato si' and Animal Well-Being: Food Ethics in a Throwaway Culture," *Journal of Catholic Social Thought* 17, no. 2 (2020): 241–60.

31 Pope Francis, "Homily of the Holy Father: Lac Ste. Anne," 26 July 2022, https://www.vatican.va/content/francesco/en/homilies/2022/documents/20220726-omelia-lacsteanne-canada.html.
32 Pope Francis, "Homily of the Holy Father: Lac Ste. Anne."
33 Brian Burkhart, *Indigenizing Philosophy through the Land: A Trickster Methodology for Decolonizing Environmental Ethics and Indigenous Futures* (East Lansing: Michigan State University Press, 2019).
34 Burkhart, *Indigenizing Philosophy*, xiv.
35 Burkhart, *Indigenizing Philosophy*, 26.
36 On what follows, see Burkhart, *Indigenizing Philosophy*, 33–42. For a complementary theological account, see Marika Rose, *Theology for the End of the World* (London: SCM Press, 2023), 177–84.
37 See Andrew Levine, *Engaging Political Philosophy from Hobbes to Rawls* (Malden, MA: Blackwell, 2002), 95–111.
38 This contingency is explicated in the corresponding paragraphs in the fifth chapter of Locke's *Second Treatise on Government*. See John Locke, *Two Treatises of Government*, ed. Peter Laslett (Cambridge, UK: Cambridge University Press, 2008), 285–93.
39 That Euro-Indigenous agreements remain within the parameters of the state of nature is stated explicitly in the second chapter of Locke's *Second Treatise on Government*. See Locke, *Two Treatises of Government*, 277.
40 Burkhart, *Indigenizing Philosophy*, 41.
41 Burkhart, *Indigenizing Philosophy*, 109–12.
42 Pope Francis, "Homily of the Holy Father: Lac Ste. Anne."
43 Paulette Regan, *Unsettling the Settler Within: Indian Residential Schools, Truth Telling, and Reconciliation in Canada* (Vancouver: UBC Press, 2010), 178.
44 Sharon Jarvis, "Michael Marker Dialogues with Francis on Primacy of Place: Advocating for Papaschase First Nation," *Journal of Contemporary Issues in Education* 18, no. 2 (2023): 85.
45 Jarvis, "Michael Marker Dialogues," 90–1.
46 See Christine Jamieson, "Pope Francis's Apology: Encounter and Meaning," *Journal of Moral Theology* 12, no. 1 (2023): 63–71.
47 Quoted in TRC, *Final Report*, vol. 6, 82.
48 Quoted in TRC, *Final Report*, vol. 6, 105.

5

The Papal Apology and Its Impacts on the Métis

Now What?

Chantal Fiola

In 2015, the Truth and Reconciliation Commission of Canada published its multi-volume final report on the legacy of the Indian residential schools, including ninety-four recommendations titled *Calls to Action*. Call 58 states, "We call upon the Pope to issue an apology to Survivors, their families, and communities for the Roman Catholic Church's role in the spiritual, cultural, emotional, physical, and sexual abuse of First Nations, Inuit, and Métis children in Catholic-run residential schools … to be delivered by the Pope in Canada."[1] Prior to the establishment of the commission in 2008, the other denominations involved in operating the schools – Anglican, Presbyterian, and United – had already apologized via the *Indian Residential Schools Settlement Agreement* (2006).[2] Finally, Pope Francis apologized on 1 April 2022 at the Vatican to First Nations, Métis, and Inuit delegations[3] and again during the pope's three-stop visit to Canada from 24 to 29 July 2022.[4]

Below, I draw on nearly two decades of research into Métis spirituality to examine critically the papal visits and apology, as well as the resulting mixed reactions from Indigenous people – especially Manitoba Métis –

including statements by the Manitoba Métis Federation's president. I conclude by calling on the Catholic Church to move meaningfully toward truth and reconciliation by undertaking the actions required to do so, including renouncing Christian supremacy and acknowledging the validity of Indigenous spirituality.

MÉTIS SPIRITUALITY

I am Michif (Red River Métis), a citizen of the Manitoba Métis Federation (MMF), with family from St Laurent, Manitoba. I am active in Métis politics, co-founded the Two-Spirit Michif Local, and served on its Executive Committee. For seventeen years, I have studied Métis relationships with ceremonies, authoring two books on the subject, and I am working on a third. During this time, I have been committed to a spiritual way of life, was initiated into the Midewiwin (or Grand Medicine Society) in 2011, and completed a four-year sun dance commitment in 2021.

My research – archival, oral history, literature, primary – debunks the stereotype that all Métis are Catholic and do not participate in Indigenous ceremonies. In *Rekindling the Sacred Fire: Métis Ancestry and Anishinaabe Spirituality* (2015),[5] I trace the colonial dispossession of Métis from our lands, culture, and ceremonies via Christianization, day and residential schools, the child welfare system, Canada outlawing ceremonies, and the requirement for us to prove that we are "wholly distinct" from First Nations in order to access rights under section 35 of the Canadian Constitution.[6] Consequently, many Métis families have become intergenerationally disconnected from ceremonies.

In *Returning to Ceremony: Spirituality in Manitoba Métis Communities*,[7] I uncover additional evidence that historically some Métis participated in ceremonies. As shown in archival correspondence, the early priests in Manitoba lamented that Métis people attended church *and* "La Grande Médécine" (Midewiwin Lodge).[8] I visited Métis elders like Maria Campbell who shared oral history on Métis participating in ceremonies. I learned about the Nêhiyaw Pwat, an early 1800s Plains Confederacy between the Nêhiyawak, Nakoda, Anishinaabeg, and Michif, and I learned about the sun dance ceremony gifted to the Michif and the Anishinaabeg in North Dakota.[9] Even Gabriel Dumont, Louis Riel's contemporary and a Métis leader in his own right, had a vision quest at puberty and became a pipe carrier and a sweat lodge conductor.[10] Moreover, Métis from six historic Manitoba Métis communities – Duck Bay, Camperville, St Laurent, St François-Xavier, Ste Anne, and Lorette – shared with me their experiences, including factors that inhibit and encourage reconnecting with ceremonies. Métis often leave their community to access ceremonies; however, Métis communities now have increasing access to ceremonies, such as the return of the sun dance in Duck Bay, MMF president David Chartrand's community.

Currently, I am project director for a study "Expressions of Métis Spirituality and Religion across the Homeland," conducted in partnership with three Métis communities, three universities across the prairie provinces, and the Rupertsland Centre for Métis Research. We are guided by a Métis Knowledge Carriers Council and by Métis community liaisons.

Across these three studies, via questionnaires, interviews, and talking circles, I have heard about the experiences of approximately three hundred Métis, many of whom participate in ceremonies, including some who identify as Christian.[11] Métis spirituality can be understood on a continuum, with Indigenous spirituality/ceremonies on one end, Christianity on the other, and syncretism in between.[12] My research confirms that *Métis spirituality has always included ceremonies*, and a spiritual resurgence is presently occurring. I bring this cumulative knowledge and experience to understanding the papal visits, apology, and impacts on Manitoba Métis.

EXAMINING THE PAPAL VISITS AND APOLOGY

The papal visits and apology are important steps in the Catholic Church's effort to make amends for the catastrophic residential school system. Indigenous (including Métis) critiques of the papal visit included the failure of the Catholic Church to take institutional accountability for its role, the refusal of the Vatican to cover the financial cost of the visits, the decision not to deliver the apology in English, the apology's exclusion of day schools, its omission of the term "genocide," Pope Francis's failure to mention sexual abuse during his first visits, and the limitations of his "repudiation" of the Doctrine of Discovery.

In the apology,[13] Pope Francis reduced the systemic genocide perpetuated by the Catholic Church to "evil" actions perpetrated by "Christian individuals."[14] He offered a qualified apology at the Vatican: "For the deplorable conduct of *those members* of the Catholic Church, I ask for God's forgiveness and I want to say to you with all my heart: I am very sorry."[15] Many expected the pope to acknowledge the Catholic Church's role as a key architect of the residential school system.

In addition to individualizing and avoiding accountability, the apologies at the Vatican and in Canada did not contain the word "genocide." Pope Francis later admitted genocide when talking with a reporter on an airplane travelling back to the Vatican. Asked why he had not used the term, he said, "I didn't use the word because it didn't come to my mind, but I described the genocide,"[16] an explanation that trivialized the genocidal system and thus minimized the culpability of the Catholic Church.

Despite his ability to speak English and French, the pope delivered inaccessible apologies in Italian at the Vatican and then Spanish while in Canada. Using English would have signalled an intent to reach the widest audience. Likewise, if the pope had not skipped the dinner and political meeting with bishops and Indigenous leaders in Quebec, he would have demonstrated contrition and willingness to reconcile.[17]

An egregious omission was the pope's failure to apologize for sexual abuse in residential schools during his statements at the Vatican and then in Maskwacis, Alberta. This omission was deliberate since the pope's statements were carefully vetted (Taylor 2022). After criticism, he mentioned sexual abuse during his Quebec statement. Also absent was mention of the ongoing crisis of child sexual abuse perpetrated by Catholic clergy and its systemic cover-up.[18]

The Government of Canada paid $55 million for what Pope Francis called his "penitential pilgrimage" to Canada,[19] and Indigenous governments paid their own expenses to visit the Vatican, adding insult to injury. It is not only shameful that the Catholic Church did not pay every cent – the latest in a history of shirking financial obligation toward survivors – but also repugnant given the Vatican's incalculable wealth.[20] That money should have been spent on the cultural and spiritual recovery and revitalization of survivors.[21]

Nearly a year after the apology and following decades of Indigenous lobbying, Pope Francis "repudiated" the Doctrine of Discovery laid out in papal bulls of the 1400s that justify colonization, dispossession, and theft of Indigenous lands.[22] He claimed that the Doctrine of Discovery was "not part of the teaching of the Catholic Church" and then mentioned the 1537 bull *Sublimis Deus*, which encourages treating non-Christians well, as supposed evidence of the church's support of human rights.[23] Truthfully, the Catholic Church used the Doctrine of Discovery to disregard human rights and to forcibly assimilate Indigenous people around the globe. According to Oxford Languages, "repudiate" means to refuse to accept or be associated with; to deny the truth or validity of; to refuse to fulfill or discharge (an agreement, obligation, or debt)."[24] *Rescinding* – to "revoke, cancel, or repeal (a law, order, or agreement)" – would have carried more legal weight, exposing the illegitimacy of Canadian sovereignty.[25]

Moreover, like the *Indian Residential Schools Settlement Agreement* (2006), the papal apology excluded day schools. Since Métis children were more likely to attend day schools – which were run by the same clergy and with similar abuses and intergenerational impacts – they were excluded from compensation under the agreement. Many Métis felt left out of the 2008 federal apology and the papal apology. Finally, Pope Francis's apology did not denounce Christian superiority or confirm that Indigenous spirituality is not subordinate.[26] These colonial views have been internalized by many Indigenous people, including some Métis political leaders.

MÉTIS REACT TO PAPAL VISITS AND APOLOGY

Métis day and residential school survivors and their families waited generations for an apology from the Catholic pope. Unfortunately, the papal visits and apology exacerbated divisions among the Manitoba Métis, laying bare the violence that colonial religion inflicts on Indigenous communities.

The papal apologies – both in Rome and in Canada – fomented division among Manitoba Métis, as Catholic Métis leadership failed to represent the diversity of spiritual experience both historically and currently among Métis. Having withdrawn from the Métis National Council in the fall of 2021, the Manitoba Métis Federation – now referring to itself as the National Government of the Red River Métis – sent a delegation of fifty-five Manitoba Métis to the Vatican three weeks after the initial Indigenous delegation.[27] Its Catholic president, David Chartrand, not only "effusively" accepted the pope's apology on behalf of Métis people, denied the culpability of the Catholic Church, and blamed individual abusers, but he also asked the pope to "revitalize" the Catholic Church among Manitoba Métis.[28]

Chartrand had offered similar messaging ahead of the Vatican visit. In his "President's Message" of 15 December 2021, he spoke of experiencing physical abuse by nuns in day school for speaking Saulteaux and public humiliation for having long hair. His mother said, "'Mano, mano, mano,' which means let it go, or leave it alone. She wouldn't fight against the Church, even if she was able to speak English."[29] He then highlighted positive relationships between the church and the Métis. This personal history leaves us to wonder about Chartrand's formative experiences with institutionalized religion, which taught him not to question church authority even when warranted and the use of public shaming as a control tactic.

In the "President's Message," Chartrand also criticized the Métis National Council:

> The Métis National Council (MNC) has been making comments in the national media, saying the Catholic Church took away the spiri-

> tuality of the Métis, robbing us of sweat lodges and drums … Remarks like this are uninformed and only serve to highlight the dangers of identity shifting … These are not our traditions – they are not Red River Métis practices and never have been.
>
> Anyone claiming they represent the Métis while also claiming drums and sweat lodges as our heritage is doing more than just distorting our identity as Métis, they are undermining the identity of our First Nations relatives. They also feed into the misconception that Indigenous Peoples in Canada are one group with interchangeable customs.[30]

Responding to the president's inflammatory statements implying that Métis who engage in ceremony are akin to raceshifters,[31] that Métis spirituality does not include ceremonies, and that to claim otherwise distorts Métis and First Nation identity,[32] I penned an article for the *Winnipeg Free Press* titled "Métis Spirituality Includes Traditional Ceremonies."[33] There, I highlight two decades of research into Métis spirituality, including the Manitoba Métis Federation's Pemmican Publications confirming that Métis spirituality includes ceremonies (Barkwell, Préfontaine, and Carrière-Acco 2006). I discuss interviews with Métis, including from Duck Bay (Chartrand's community), and conclude by noting that Chartrand's statements erase the contributions of our maternal relations (First Nations and then Métis) who taught us these spiritual traditions, which arguably amounts to misogyny.

Similarly, a friend texted me on 23 September 2023 from the Infinity Women's Secretariat Annual General Meeting to inform me, "Chartrand is talking about you again." This friend quoted him as saying, "There's a Métis university professor who got mad at me. She tried to say First Nations ceremony is part of our culture, but I told her it wasn't. Some people participate, sure, but it's not ours. *So, she wrote a book because she was mad at me.*"[34] He continued this line of commentary at the MMF Annual General Assembly.

On 13 October 2023, day 1 of the assembly, I received a text message from a friend informing me that Chartrand was yet again talking about my research.[35] At the assembly, as I saw when I watched a recording of the proceedings, a former MMF employee tried to discredit the "new Métis research academic journal" – a reference to *Pawaatamihk: Journal of Métis Thinkers* – for not including the MMF as a "stakeholder" yet promoting itself as "nation-specific."[36] The speaker concluded, "When research is done about us, without our collective consent, that research can lead to misrepresentation and misrecognition … including raceshifting."[37] President Chartrand responded, "This is a serious issue. It's no different than identity theft." He said that the MMF was "establishing a body because we're having authors out there that are writing, and some Métis authors too, like this one author [Chantal Fiola]." Speaking of ceremony, he then reiterated, "That's not our culture. That's not our history." He added that the MMF was "actually creating a body … [to] look at all of the books that are coming out, being taught in our schools … *For the Métis authors out there, you know, be careful what you're writing, be careful what you're selling, be careful what you're saying* … If it's real, [the MMF will] stamp it and say, 'This is good history. You can teach it in the schools.'"[38]

On day 3 of the assembly, in an effort to respect spiritual diversity and to separate church from state, a resolution was proposed to remove Christian prayer from the MMF's official proceedings, to be replaced by "a secular and inclusive opening or moment of reflection that welcomes attendees from all religious, spiritual, or non-religious backgrounds."[39] A spirited discussion ensued, and then the emcee permitted President Chartrand the final words before closing the discussion despite protest. Chartrand's eight-minute speech concluded,

> I will die a Christian. I will be buried a Christian. I'll have prayer at my grave … We have embraced [Christian prayer] into our Constitution, into our positions of local meetings, regional meetings, and our annual assemblies … and as far as I'm President, will always be. No matter what you vote or what you do. If this were to ever pass, I will give my resignation tomorrow morning … [Slams fist on podium, shouting] All the things we fought for, everything we have done is believed in God! … You'll never change the way we do [Christian] prayers in this assembly and in this government. Not in

> this time. Not ten years from now. Not twenty years from now. Not fifty years from now. I'll never support this![40]

Unsurprisingly, the resolution was defeated.

President Chartrand conflates the issue of Indigenous identity fraud with legitimate Métis research and publications that he simply disagrees with. Threatening *Métis authors* (not raceshifters) reveals his true agenda: censorship and upholding a patriarchal narrative of Métis identity. Silencing Métis who participate in ceremony, threatening to resign if Christian prayer is removed from MMF business (i.e., imposing Christianity on Métis citizens), and threatening dissenters[41] are abuses of authority made more concerning now that the MMF claims to represent all Red River Métis, including beyond Manitoba.

In political ideology, an ultranationalist government that blurs church and state, censors research and publication, silences dissent, and expects devotion to an authoritarian, dictatorial leader describes *fascism*. This dangerous, anti-intellectual stance disregards academic freedom, undermines democracy, and dishonours Métis self-determination. Given the life-affirming benefits of going to ceremony[42] and the fact that Métis participated in the past and increasingly participate in the present, it is shameful that the president of the MMF sows discord rather than respect for diversity. If the pope's apology had denounced Christian supremacy and honoured Indigenous spirituality, it may have prevented President Chartrand from weaponizing Christianity to antagonize and divide Métis citizens. An inclusive apology recognizing religious pluralism would have empowered Métis citizens to walk the spiritual path that resonates with them – without division and enmity.

MEANINGFUL TRUTH AND RECONCILIATION

If the pope and Catholic adherents are sincere in their desire for reconciliation, then truth telling and apologies must be paired with concrete actions. To conclude, I identify several outstanding actions.

Pope Leo XIV must acknowledge the role of the Catholic Church as a key architect of the genocidal day and residential school system and of the harms inflicted on (Métis) children in day schools, extending the papal apology to (Métis) survivors of day schools and their families as well as compensating them.

The pope must confess to the ongoing epidemic of child sexual abuse perpetrated by Catholic clergy and to the church's systemic cover-up of this abuse, immediately bringing all perpetrators to justice. Catholic churches must release all documents pertaining to this global crisis (while protecting survivors' confidentiality) and must cease fighting against Indigenous people in court.

The pope must admit the Catholic Church's role in the vilification and suppression of Indigenous spirituality, *including Métis participation in ceremonies.* The institution must investigate its archives and make publicly available all documentation regarding religious assimilation forced on Indigenous people and the latter's efforts to resist, noting dates, places, and other relevant details. The pope must identify ongoing assimilation efforts – including nonconsensual missionary work, evangelization, conversion, and the belief in Christian superiority – *and must immediately cease these harmful practices.*

The pope must go beyond repudiation by rescinding/revoking the Doctrine of Discovery, must acknowledge the illegitimacy of sovereignty claims based on this doctrine, and must honour Indigenous sovereignty. The Catholic Church must admit all theft of Indigenous lands and promptly return them.

The Catholic Church must fulfill all financial obligations to survivors of abuse at day and residential schools, including those obligations that the church has been prematurely released from, and must pay any compensation needed to make full reparations for its crimes related to Indigenous people, paying all costs associated with these actions. The Catholic Church must use its incalculable wealth – accumulated via the global dispossession and oppression of Indigenous Peoples – to implement the Truth and Reconciliation Commission's *Calls to Action* (2015).

Finally, the Catholic Church and its adherents must affirm the legitimacy and value of those spiritualities that have been brutally repressed. It must disavow Christian supremacy, and it must advance theologies that encourage its leaders, including politicians such as Chartrand, to embrace religious pluralism in all contexts but especially in those where Christianity was imposed through genocidal practices.

If the Christian churches, which comprise the largest institutionalized religion in the world – with 2.3 billion Christians,[43] 1.36 billion of whom are Catholic[44] – undertake this work, intergenerational healing will ensue for all. Anyone who thinks that it is unreasonable or unrealistic to expect the above actions to be taken should ask themselves whether it is reasonable or realistic for the Catholic Church to reconcile with Indigenous Peoples and to make amends for the unfathomable intergenerational damage inflicted on Indigenous sovereignty and people. Time will reveal whether the Catholic Church, its thousands of churches, and its billions of adherents choose to enact ongoing colonial religious assimilation or to become good relatives on earth.

NOTES

1 Truth and Reconciliation Commission of Canada (TRC), *Calls to Action* (2015), no. 58, https://www2.gov.bc.ca/assets/gov/british-columbians-our-governments/indigenous-people/aboriginal-peoples-documents/calls_to_action_english2.pdf.

2 Government of Canada, *Indian Residential Schools Settlement Agreement* (2006), https://www.rcaanc-cirnac.gc.ca/eng/1100100015576/1571581687074.

3 Pope Francis, "Address of His Holiness Pope Francis: Clementine Hall," 1 April 2022, https://www.vatican.va/content/francesco/en/speeches/2022/april/documents/20220401-popoli-indigeni-canada.html.

4 Vatican, "Apostolic Journey of His Holiness Pope Francis to Canada, 24–30 July 2022," 23 June 2022, https://www.vatican.va/content/francesco/en/travels/2022/outside/documents/canada-2022.html.

5 Chantal Fiola, *Rekindling the Sacred Fire: Metis Ancestry and Anishinaabe Spirituality* (Winnipeg: University of Manitoba Press, 2015).

6 Martha McCarthy, *To Evangelize the Nations: Roman Catholic Missions in Manitoba, 1818–1870* (Winnipeg: Manitoba Culture Heritage and Recreation Historic Resources, 1990); Larry Chartrand, Tricia Logan, and Harry Daniels, eds, *Métis History and Experience and Residential Schools in Canada* (Ottawa: Aboriginal Healing Foundation, 2006); Katherine Pettipas, *Severing the Ties That Bind: Government Repression of Indigenous Religious Ceremonies on the Prairies* (Winnipeg: University of Manitoba Press, 1994).

7 Chantal Fiola, *Returning to Ceremony: Spirituality in Manitoba Métis Communities* (Winnipeg: University of Manitoba Press, 2021).

8 Charles Camper to Alexandre-Antonin Taché, Mission de St Laurent, Lac Manitoba, 12 September 1868, Collection les Cloches de St-Boniface, Centre du patrimoine de la Société historique du Saint-Boniface, Winnipeg; Laurent Simonet to Alexandre-Antonin Taché, Mission de St-Laurent, Lac Manitoba, 2 April 1866, Collection les Cloches de St-Boniface, Centre du patrimoine de la Société historique du Saint-Boniface, Winnipeg.

9 Lawrence Barkwell, Darren Préfontaine, and Anne Carrière-Acco, "Metis Spirituality," in *Metis Legacy II: Michif Culture, Heritage and Folkways*, ed. Lawrence Barkwell, Leah Dorion, and Audreen Hourie, 184–6 (Saskatoon and Winnipeg: Gabriel Dumont Institute and Pemmican, 2006); Nicholas Vrooman, "Many Eagle Set Thirsty Dance (Sun Dance) Song: The Métis Receive Sun Dance Song," in *Metis Legacy II: Michif Culture, Heritage and Folkways*, ed. Lawrence Barkwell, Leah Dorion, and Audreen Hourie, 187–91 (Saskatoon and Winnipeg: Gabriel Dumont Institute and Pemmican, 2006).

10 Charles Duncan Thompson, *Red Sun: Gabriel Dumont, the Folk Hero* (Saskatoon: Gabriel Dumont Institute Press, 2017).

11 Herein, I focus on Métis who engage in ceremony. My current project will result in a book that broadens this discussion to include Christian Métis.

12 Fiola, *Returning to Ceremony*.

13 Pope Francis, "Address of His Holiness: Maskwacis," 25 July 2022,

https://www.vatican.va/content/francesco/en/speeches/2022/july/documents/20220725-popolazioniindigene-canada.html. See also Canadian Press, "'I am deeply sorry': Full Text of Residential School Apology from Pope Francis," CBC *News*, 25 July 2022, https://www.cbc.ca/news/canada/edmonton/pope-francis-maskwacis-apology-full-text-1.6531341.

14 Canadian Press, "'He Took Ownership': Manitoba Métis Meet with Pope Francis at the Vatican," *Winnipeg CityNews*, 22 April 2022, https://winnipeg.citynews.ca/2022/04/21/manitoba-metis-meet-with-pope-francis-at-the-vatican/.

15 Pope Francis, "Address of His Holiness Pope Francis: Clementine Hall," emphasis added. See also Shari Narine, "Métis Delegation for Audience with Pope Focuses on Moving forward with Catholic Church," *Toronto Star*, 22 April 2022, https://www.thestar.com/news/canada/m-tis-delegation-for-audience-with-pope focuses-on-moving-forward-with-catholic-church/article_d2fbea34-3a7c-5880-9a1c-126de50b0617.html.

16 Pope Francis, "Press Conference on the Return Flight to Rome," 29 July 2022, https://www.vatican.va/content/francesco/en/speeches/2022/july/documents/20220729-voloritorno-canada.html. See also Ka'nhehsí:io Deer, "Pope Says Genocide Took Place at Canada's Residential Schools," *CBC News*, 30 July 2022, https://www.cbc.ca/news/indigenous/pope-francis-residential-schools-genocide-1.6537203.

17 Emelia Fournier and Lindsay Richardson, "Meeting between First Nation Chiefs and Bishops 'Missed Opportunity' says Cree Leader." APTN *News*, 29 July 2022, https://www.aptnnews.ca/national-news/meeting-between-first-nation-chiefs-and-bishops-missed-opportunity-says-cree-leader/.

18 Pamela Palmater cites a commission, an inquiry, and a report – dated between 2017 and 2021– that respectively found 4,445 victims sexually abused in an Australian Catholic setting between the 1950s and the 1980s, 216,000 victims of sexual abuse perpetrated by 3,000 French Catholic clergy between 1950 and 2020, and 1,700 Catholic clergy "credibly accused of child sexual abuse" living in easy access of children. Catholic policy includes systemic cover-up, failure to report or expel perpetrators, and "church abuse and molestation" liability insurance. Pamela Palmater, "Another Pope's Apology Isn't Enough When Catholic: Church's Cover-ups

and Hypocrisy Continue to This Day," *Toronto Star*, 24 July 2022, https://pampalmater.com/wp-content/uploads/2022/08/Another-popes-apology-isnt-enough-when-Churchs-shameful-acts-continue-_-The-Star.pdf.

19 Pope Francis, "Angelus," 17 July 2022, https://www.vatican.va/content/francesco/en/angelus/2022/documents/20220717-angelus.html.

20 In 2006, forty-nine Catholic entities agreed to raise $25 million to compensate residential school survivors but were released by the courts after raising only $4 million. In 2021, the Canadian Conference of Catholic Bishops committed $30 million over five years. Kelly Geraldine Malone, "Pope Francis' Tour Came with a Minimum $55 Million Price Tag for Ottawa," CTV *News*, 23 March 2023, https://www.ctvnews.ca/politics/pope-francis-tour-came-with-a-minimum-55-million-price-tag-for-ottawa-1.6325266. The Catholic Church has not upheld these financial commitments despite the Vatican generating $887 million in 2022 and having $37 *billion* in assets. Janet Nguyen, "How Much Money Does 'God' Have?" *Marketplace*, 11 February 2023, https://www.marketplace.org/2023/02/10/how-much-money-does-catholic-church-have/; Vinze Valeza, "The Finances behind the Vatican," *Economics Review at New York University*, 2 March 2023, https://theeconreview.com/2023/03/02/the-finances-behind-the-vatican/.

21 Malone, "Pope Francis' Tour."

22 Nicole Winfield, "Indigenous Leaders Hope Vatican's Repudiation of Oppressive Colonial Concepts Leads to Real Change," CBC *News*, 30 March 2023, https://www.cbc.ca/news/canada/vatican-reject-discovery-doctrine-indigenous-demands-1.6795728.

23 Holy See Press Office, "Joint Statement of the Dicasteries for Culture and Education and for Promoting Integral Human Development on the 'Doctrine of Discovery,'" 30 March 2023, paras 6 and 8, https://press.vatican.va/content/salastampa/en/bollettino/pubblico/2023/03/30/230330b.html. See also "Church Defends Indigenous Peoples: 'Doctrine of Discovery' Was Never Catholic," *Vatican News*, 30 March 2023, https://www.vaticannews.va/en/vatican-city/news/2023-03/vatican-formally-repudiates-doctrine-of-discovery.html.

24 Oxford University Press, "Repudiate," Oxford Languages, https://www.google.com/search?q=repudiate.

25 Oxford University Press, "Rescind," Oxford Languages, https://www.google.com/search?q=rescind.

26 Pope Francis, "Address of His Holiness: Maskwacis."

27 Olivia Stefanovich, "Manitoba Métis Leader to Ask Pope Francis to Bless Louis Riel's Grave," CBC *News*, 20 April 2022, https://www.cbc.ca/news/politics/manitoba-metis-delegation-meets-pope-francis-1.6424899.

28 Narine, "Métis Delegation for Audience"; Dave Baxter, "Manitoba Métis Federation Meets Pope, Invite Him to Ancestral Lands," *Winnipeg Sun*, 21 April 2022, https://www.winnipegsun.com/news/provincial/manitoba-metis-federation-meets-pope-invite-him-to-ancestral-lands/article_f29afff5-6636-573c-84ac-f879d788d8c7.html.

29 David Chartrand, "President's Message," Manitoba Métis Federation, 15 December 2021, https://www.mmf.mb.ca/presidents-message/presidents-message-december-15-2021.

30 Chartrand, "President's Message."

31 The term "raceshifters" is often used in reference to people who falsely claim an Indigenous identity.

32 On cultural similarities between Anishinaabe, Nêhiyaw, and Michif peoples, see Fiola, *Returning to Ceremony*; and Rob Innes, "Challenging a Racist Fiction: A Closer Look at Métis–First Nations Relations," in *A People and a Nation: New Directions in Contemporary Métis Studies*, ed. Jennifer Adese and Chris Andersen, 92–114 (Vancouver: UBC Press).

33 Chantal Fiola, "Métis Spirituality Includes Traditional Ceremonies," *Winnipeg Free Press*, 3 January 2022, https://www.winnipegfreepress.com/arts-and-life/life/faith/2022/01/03/metis-spirituality-includes-traditional-ceremonies.

34 Emphasis added. At the time, I was hosting a gathering in the Métis community of Lebret, Saskatchewan, for my current study.

35 Perhaps Chartrand is referring to John Longhurst, "Journey Leads back to Métis Spiritual Roots," *Winnipeg Free Press*, 4 December 2021, https://www.winnipegfreepress.com/arts-and-life/life/faith/2021/12/04/journey-leads-back-to-metis-spiritual-roots. In this article, Longhurst wonders whether Cassidy Caron, then president of the Métis National Council, will "tell the Pope how Métis people lost their spirituality through their interactions with the church – traditional practices like

ceremonies, dances, drumming, sweat lodges." I am interviewed for the remainder of the article.

36 Manitoba Métis Federation, "MMF Annual General Assembly: Day 1," *YouTube*, 13 October 2023, 5:27:53 to 5:27:59, https://www.youtube.com/watch?v=KiQYScsmeJ8. The full exchange between the former MMF employee and Chartrand is at 5:23:59 to 5:35:30.

37 Manitoba Métis Federation, "MMF Annual General Assembly: Day 1," 5:28:11. Alternatives to securing ethics approval from Indigenous governments (e.g., community elders' councils) when warranted are outlined in Government of Canada, "Research Involving First Nations, Inuit, and Métis Peoples of Canada," in *Tri-Council Policy Statement: Ethical Conduct for Research Involving Humans* (2022), arts 9.5, 9.6, 9.7, https://ethics.gc.ca/eng/policy-politique_tcps2-eptc2_2022.html. I obtained MMF ethics approval for *Returning to Ceremony*, but it is dangerous to imply that ethical Métis research and publication cannot exist beyond MMF control or that research conducted without MMF approval is not *Métis*.

38 Manitoba Métis Federation, "MMF Annual General Assembly: Day 1," 5:35:20, emphasis added. In response, Dr Laura Forsythe – a member of *Pawaatamihk*'s Circle of Editors, which includes myself and others – clarified that all authors submit their Community Statement (indicating citizenship, etc.) and undergo peer review by Métis scholars and that all of the journal's editors are Métis citizens (5:37:06 to 5:38:50).

39 Manitoba Métis Federation, "MMF Annual General Assembly: Day 3," *YouTube*, 15 October 2023, 6:32:32 to 6:32:45, https://www.youtube.com/watch?v=V2Fp26kTkrA.

40 Manitoba Métis Federation, "MMF Annual General Assembly: Day 3," 6:58:00 to 7:04:18.

41 For example, at the MMF's Annual General Assembly in 2024, in response to a university local member's social media post encouraging citizens to support a resolution asking the MMF's cabinet to denounce the ongoing genocide against Palestinian people, President Chartrand threatened, "I'll go out there and beat the shit out of anybody that comes and tries to threaten my people." Ozten Shebahkeget, "Manitoba Métis Federation President's Remark in Heated Debate on Israel-Hamas War Sparks

Concern," CBC *News*, 31 October 2024, https://www.cbc.ca/news/canada/manitoba/mmf-chartrand-assembly-israel-resolution-1.7366696.

42 Michael Chandler and Christopher Lalonde, "Cultural Continuity as a Hedge against Suicide in Canada's First Nations," *Transcultural Psychiatry* 35, no. 2 (1998): 191–219.

43 Pew Research Centre, "Religious Composition by Country, 2010–2020," 9 June 2025, https://www.pewresearch.org/religion/interactives/religious-composition-by-country-2010-2050/.

44 Nguyen, "How Much Money?"

6

The Political Practice of Canadian Church Apologies to Indigenous Peoples

Jeremy M. Bergen

The apology for Indian residential schools made by Pope Francis in 2022 during what he called his "penitential pilgrimage" to Canada[1] may be understood as a response to the *Calls to Action* published by the Truth and Reconciliation Commission of Canada (TRC) in 2015.[2] Grouped under the heading "Church Apologies and Reconciliation," calls 58 through 61 ask churches to take specific actions related to education, respect for Indigenous spirituality, and ongoing funding. Yet none of the other churches that ran schools were called to apologize, likely because they had already made such statements decades earlier. Despite singling out an apology from the pope, the TRC's calls to the churches are premised on the value of such apologies to the *political* practices of truth and of reconciliation, especially to the reorienting of relationships between churches and Indigenous Peoples. In this chapter, I situate the papal apologies in the context of other apologies by Canadian churches, including Canadian Catholic entities, and show how these apologies may be understood as political practice. Drawing on the work of Canadian philosopher Alice MacLachlan and Australian sociologist Danielle Celermajer,

I use the lens of political practice to illuminate some of the promises and the challenges of church apologies for Indian residential schools.

I write as a white-settler Christian theologian in Canada with some expertise on church apologies for historical wrongs. My own Mennonite ancestors settled on dispossessed Indigenous lands of Treaties 1 and 7, and I now live on the Haldimand Tract in Ontario. My late grandfather served for one year as a teacher in the Indian day school run by the United Church of Canada in Cross Lake, Manitoba, to which he was assigned as his alternative service as a conscientious objector during the Second World War. Mennonites ran several residential schools in Ontario.[3] Although I am tempted to minimize and qualify some of these connections – for instance, the day school was on reserve, and thus children were not separated from their families in the same way that they were at residential schools; and the Mennonite-affiliated residential schools were not directly run by the denomination of which I am a member – I take critical notice of such impulses as "settler moves to innocence." By that phrase, Eve Tuck and K. Wayne Yang refer to "those strategies or positionings that attempt to relieve the settler of feelings of guilt or responsibility without giving up land or power or privilege, without having to change much at all."[4] Nevertheless, the analysis that I offer is intended to advance justice, repair, reconciliation, and healing.

The church parties to the *Indian Residential Schools Settlement Agreement* (2006)[5] were the Anglican Church of Canada (ACC), the Presbyterian Church in Canada (PCC), the United Church of Canada (UCC),[6] and various Roman Catholic entities.[7] Here, I provide a brief overview of their apologies prior to the agreement.[8]

Advocacy by Indigenous leaders within the UCC led its 1986 General Council to authorize an apology that was delivered by moderator the Rt Rev. Robert Smith inside a teepee on the grounds of Laurentian University, where the council meetings were being held. His words, addressed to Indigenous members of the church, focused on the historic failure of the church to respect Indigenous voices and spirituality, instead imposing "our civilization as a condition of accepting the gospel." The statement did not name residential schools or the dispossession of land but focused instead on how, in the words of the moderator, "we tried to make you be like us."[9]

The issue of residential schools came to the Canadian public agenda in the 1990s, partly due to the public disclosure by the national chief of the Assembly of First Nations, Phil Fontaine, that he had been abused at a residential school and partly due to subsequent lawsuits by survivors of abuse at some schools. The president of the Oblate Conference of Canada, Fr Douglas, OMI, Crosby, on behalf of the Missionary Oblates of Mary Immaculate, which ran the majority of Catholic schools, made a statement of apology in 1991.[10] This statement made a clear distinction between two issues sometimes conflated in public discourse – on the one hand, the very existence of the schools as a tool of a policy of assimilation reflective of attitudes of religious imperialism and, on the other hand, the abuse of students, including criminal physical and sexual abuse – and apologized for each. Crosby delivered the statement at the Lac Ste Anne Pilgrimage Grounds, a significant site of gathering for Indigenous people, which Pope Francis would visit in 2022.

The ACC's landmark apology was made by its primate, Archbishop Michael Peers, in 1993. At the end of a week spent listening to the stories of survivors at the Native Convocation of the Anglican Church, Peers asked to address the group. Highly personal, with several "I" statements – "I have heard … I accept … I know" – but delivered on behalf of the church, the apology acknowledged the many failures of the churches and pledged "to walk with you along the path of God's healing," a promise addressed both to those in the room and to Indigenous Anglicans more broadly. A formula repeated three times – "I am sorry, more than I can say, that …" – acknowledged the inadequacy of words, a not uncommon feature of public apologies, and offered them nevertheless.[11]

The PCC's "Confession" was approved by a general assembly in 1994, unlike the other statements discussed so far, which were written by leaders authorized and delegated to do so. As a consequence, there was more debate about the specific wording, including how the "good faith" intentions of Presbyterians who worked in the schools would be acknowledged. The approved statement addressed three audiences: it spoke to the PCC's churches/members, it asked God for forgiveness, and it asked forgiveness of all "Aboriginal peoples," not just those who are in the church.[12] This orientation was expressed when the confession was publicly presented to National Chief Phil Fontaine.

In 1998, the UCC faced a significant lawsuit from survivors of abuse at one particular school and feared more to come. Despite this litigation, and in response to growing grassroots pressure, moderator the Rt Rev. Bill Phipps made a public statement of apology on behalf of the UCC. Building on the more general 1986 apology, he focused on the church's complicity in the system of assimilation, as well as on the physical, sexual, and mental abuse experienced by students. He also addressed those within the UCC who did not understand why such apologies for the past were necessary and appropriate, an audience that is in fact important in all of these apologies.[13]

Following the detection in May 2021 of the unmarked graves of 215 children at the former Catholic-run Kamloops Indian Residential School, public pressure intensified for the pope to deliver an apology. Despite a 2018 statement from the Canadian Conference of Catholic Bishops (CCCB) that the pope "could not personally respond" to call 58 of the TRC's *Calls to Action*,[14] along with public statements by a prominent archbishop that a "dramatic" gesture such as a papal apology would not be the best way to pursue reconciliation,[15] pressure continued to mount. Catholic leaders had asserted that the appropriate authorities had already apologized. In addition to the Oblate apology, several bishops had apologized in the 1990s on behalf of their dioceses that ran particular schools.[16] Other apologies were made as statements during the proceedings of the TRC or in the aftermath of the Kamloops discovery. In a statement on its website explaining why there would not be an apology from the Catholic Church in Canada, the CCCB explained, "Each diocese and religious community is corporately and legally responsible for its own actions. The Catholic Church as a whole in Canada was not associated with the Residential Schools, nor was the Canadian Conference of Catholic Bishops."[17]

Yet the calls for acknowledgment and apology were not primarily about legal responsibility or interested in the nuance of institutional structures.

The call was for the Catholic Church to take moral and spiritual responsibility and to cease deflecting. The claim that the "Catholic Church as a whole in Canada" did not run residential schools not only demanded that survivors accept an official Catholic version of what happened and who did the harm but also denied the widespread experience that the responsible party was simply the "Catholic Church." Indigenous people, not Catholic authorities, would determine that an adequate apology needed to come from the pope – the one who could speak for the whole.

The scholarly discourse on public and collective apologies has accelerated since the 1990s, reflecting a substantial increase in statements of apology by various political actors.[18] Early work by Nicholas Tavuchis and by Aaron Lazare drew on the dynamics of personal apology in order to account for collective apology, such as those by states.[19] Various volumes examine how apologies have been deployed to address historical injustices and to negotiate conflicts.[20] Scholars offer a range of assessments, including criteria of assessment for authentic political apologies.[21] Apologies for the Indian residential schools in Canada have been seen primarily through the lens of Prime Minister Stephen Harper's 2008 apology.[22]

Within the multidisciplinary discourse on apologies, those by churches are occasionally noted in passing but not typically considered in their own right. Canadian church apologies for residential schools have been analyzed from the perspectives of rhetoric, religious ethics, peace studies, and church history.[23] In my academic book on the subject, I analyze dozens of such church apologies and propose a theological framework for understanding the coherence and meaning of this relatively recent practice.[24] In a subsequent scholarly article, I propose practical considerations for church entities contemplating public apologies, drawing primarily on the examples related to the Indian residential schools.[25] One scholar proposes how a theology of apology might help to decolonize Roman Catholic practice and identity in Canada.[26]

Alice MacLachlan's analysis of "political apologies" focuses primarily on public statements by nations, although she acknowledges that apologies by leaders of corporations, churches, and nongovernmental organizations may also be political in the senses that she describes. She warns against using the norms of the personal apology to determine the nature and meaning of political apologies. She furthermore cautions against the use of abstract regulative ideals to determine what constitutes a genuine apology. Rather, drawing on Hannah Arendt's work, she proposes that political apologies be interpreted as political practice. For Arendt, political practices generate their own principles and standards, often ones that render the very conditions that make political life (and thus political speech) possible in the first place.[27]

MacLachlan highlights several implications, which I summarize as four significant aspects relevant for Canadian church apologies. First, political apologies are public; they take place in a "shared 'space of appearance'" and are "made with an eye to the spectators of history."[28] Second, such an apology "discloses the agent who speaks, in ways she may not be able to control."[29] An apology raises questions about the very identity of the entity that speaks, both with respect to a problematic past ("we did not act as we believe a church should act") and with respect to how apologetic speech may be meaningful displayed in the present ("we can rightfully speak to actions that were taken generations earlier"). However, what an apology means is not controlled by the speaker but by how an apology is received, which may be according to standards that the speaker does not like.

Third, as political speech, church apologies authorize particular stories about the past and the present. Part of this effect is achieved by putting on the record in ritually appropriate ways an account by authorized representatives. Residential schools *were* part of the Canadian policy of assimilation and, as a result, were part of a policy that churches now denounce. These stories may be designed to communicate somewhat differently to different audiences – such as survivors and their families, Indigenous persons who are part of a particular church, and those of the dominant culture on whose behalf the statements are made. Fourth, apologies may occasion and advance relational change. They may speak about change, for example, in the form of promises, but they may also symbolize and embody new relationships. For example, for all its shortcomings, Harper's apology was lauded for breaking with protocol to permit Indigenous leaders to give responses in the House of Commons as part of the official record.

Danielle Celermajer explains the political dimensions of church apologies primarily through the concept of "recovenanting," the religious resonance of which points not only to the quasi-religious dimension in apologies by nations but also to the political dimension of church apologies. Jewish ideas about covenants with God include collective repentance in which "the people," such as on Yom Kippur, repent of collective wrongdoing and recommit to the ethical obligations at the core of their identity as a people in relation to God. National apologies are also about the basic identity of the nation and about its ethical values and commitments as might be expressed not in religious texts but in constitutions and charters of rights and freedoms.[30]

The national apologies to Indigenous people that Celermajer examines perform recovenanting work through a complex process that is ultimately forward-looking. A national apology must affirm that the agent now speaking is both the agent that perpetrated the wrong and the agent that now condemns the wrong. It does so in the name of commitment to particular values, such as inclusion and justice, which it declares to be essential to its identity, even if these values were not fully recognized in the past. The notion of collective responsibility on which such an apology is premised leads Celermajer to address two arguments made against the legitimacy of apologies for the past, namely that they blame the wrong people (i.e., those speaking the apology were not the perpetrators) and that they inappropriately judge the past by the standards of the present.[31] Although individuals in the present may not have personal or criminal liability for past policies or abuses, they ought to make judgments about the past for the sake of the future. In order to affirm particular ethical norms as foundational for the very identity of the nation, it is necessary to name their violation and commit to their repair. There may be some element of a return to foundational principles, as implied by the religious concept of repentance, but Celermajer also acknowledges that certain aspirations may not have been realized in the past in order for them to be present expressions of identity by which past failures are judged. Positive

Indigenous-settler relations may be an ethical value yet to be fulfilled. In this sense, apologies are not about the past per se but about referring to the past for the sake of a future ethical collective identity. Such an apology is a political act of "recovenanting the nation."[32]

The apologies issued by Canadian churches in the 1980s and 1990s, as well the apologies of Pope Francis in 2022,[33] may all be understood as political acts of recovenanting. Through such apologies, churches navigate their very identities as churches that have betrayed their callings yet remain the churches responsible to work to repair the harms. As churches repent or apologize, they express new commitments to relationships with Indigenous people that better reflect the very identity and calling of the church. The apologies themselves serve the important function of providing a way for these churches to articulate their identities while making specific ethical and political commitments to the future.

First, these apologies provide an authoritative narrative about the past. They seek to put on the public record a truth about the past, not in all its details but in a general way intended to stake out a basic moral position and to exclude forms of denial. Pope Francis acknowledged how the policy of assimilation that sought to destroy Indigenous identities, languages, cultures, and spirituality was part of a larger process of colonization. Although some apologies add the nuance that people with good intentions served in the schools, which may be read as justifying or minimizing the harms caused, these qualifications are contextualized by an overwhelming denunciation, for which the church may now be held accountable by others.

Second, these apologies disclose the ecclesial identities of the agents speaking. Here, there is a significant difference between Catholic and Protestant practices of apology. Pope Francis followed the pattern of Pope John Paul II, in which the pope asks for pardon in the name of the church but for the wrongs of individual members of the church just as a mother (or Mother Church) asks for pardon for her wayward children.[34] The pope did not acknowledge that the Catholic Church as an institution was responsible for implementing a harmful, let alone sinful, policy. Rather, it was the responsibility of "a number of Catholics, particularly those with educational responsibilities,"[35] along with those "many Christians [who] supported the colonizing mentality of the powers that oppressed the Indigenous people."[36] The pope acknowledged that structural injustice was embodied and advanced by institutions such as the government but did not acknowledge the role of the church per se.

Although there are theological reasons for this formulation, there are significant voices within Catholic theology calling for more explicit acknowledgment of the sinfulness of the church.[37] From the perspective on how Catholic apologies will be received by the public, the political character of these statements presses official Catholic apologies to make explicit what is already implied by them. The public will judge an apology through the lens of whether the appropriate agent – the church – has taken responsibility and, even more importantly, whether this agent's understanding of the harm that it has caused is such that the institution itself will take appropriate collective action. A public audience will not and does not believe a story about a sinless institution. Unless there is acknowledgment of failures (and sin) at the institutional level, there is little reason to expect that institutional action and reforms will be undertaken to repair the damage and to ensure that such acts are not repeated in the future. By contrast, the apologies of the UCC, PCC, and ACC clearly identify the church as the agent that implemented harmful policies and failed to protect children from abuse. In doing so, these apologies more clearly and compellingly communicate that the church itself needs to change in order to bring about repair.

Third, church apologies seek to constitute a communal identity by way of ethical commitments that are supported and advanced by a church's many members. To this end, church apologies as political practice seek to educate and persuade church members of the rightness of words that have already been spoken on their behalf. The collective, such as a nation or a church, exists not only as a unified entity on whose behalf authorized leaders may speak and take action but also as the sum of its many members. Political apologies are apologies by representatives on behalf of the whole, but part of their purpose is to bring about a reconstituted identity that supports reparative action at various levels. Addressing non-Indigenous church members is evident in efforts to publicize the apology and to provide resources for its reception at the local level, such as the production of videos, study guides, tours by Indigenous and church leaders, and acts of remembrance on important anniversaries.

Pope Francis explicitly encouraged "the Bishops and the Catholic community to continue taking steps towards the transparent search for truth and to foster healing and reconciliation."[38] He called on individual Christians to "grow in the ability to accept and respect the identity and experience of indigenous peoples," a process that he said must "penetrate hearts."[39] UCC moderator Phipps addressed skeptics in his own church who did not believe that the church was now responsible for the sins of the past by explaining, "The truth is, we are the bearers of many blessings from our ancestors, and therefore, we must also bear their burdens."[40]

The failure to prepare members and to foster ownership for an apology statement is most evident in the backlash to the 1991 Oblate apology. Few members of the order had been expecting the statement, and many were caught by surprise. There was a backlash among former staff who did not appreciate the statements supposedly made on their behalf. As a result, the Oblate president issued a second apology in which he acknowledged the failure to adequately consult and provide adequate warning about the statement.[41] Despite the fact that the initial Oblate apology offered a caveat about the "sincere and heroic" dedication of many who served in the school, a sentiment alluded to in the PCC statement but otherwise absent in the others, the backlash indicates the importance of laying groundwork for the reaction to an apology by those on whose behalf it is made.

Fourth, apologies navigate a complicated relationship with control. On the one hand, the speaker commands public attention. They may use the opportunity to control the narrative about the past, minimize the wrongs of the past, frame their own efforts to repair, and demand certain kinds of responses from victims. On the other hand, the speaker's renunciation of control may be the most significant indicator of a genuine understanding of the harms caused, of the need for profound institutional changes, and of the willingness to address the needs of victims/survivors. The apology event may be a microcosm of some shift in power relations.

It is this risk that makes it political practice in the sense that MacLachlan describes. Both dynamics are evident among Canadian church apologies.

In the 1990s, the UCC was advised that a statement of *repentance* for residential schools would not expose it to legal liability in the way that an *apology* would. In 1997, it took the safer route and offered a statement of repentance. After criticism from survivors and from UCC members, the church made a statement of apology a year later in full awareness of the legal and financial risks.[42] An analysis of the wording of the repentance would not reveal it, but as the larger context makes clear, the statement was an attempt at control rather than an unconditional confession of wrongdoing.

The gap between church intention and public reception may cause churches either to relinquish some control or to assert it. On the one hand, church statements are often reported in the public media as "apologies," and judged as such, even when they intentionally avoid this nontheological language. On the other hand, such reception may enable a church to benefit from appearing to apologize according to public standards despite retaining plausible deniability, for legal or theological reasons, that it has done so. That was true of Pope Benedict XVI's 2009 private statement of "regret" to the national chief of the Assembly of First Nations, Phil Fontaine, which was reported as an apology and which some Catholic commentators later claimed had been accepted by Fontaine as an apology.[43]

In the Vatican and Maskwacis apologies, Pope Francis asks for God's forgiveness and for the pardon of those persons hearing his words.[44] (The two UCC apologies and the PCC apology also make reference to forgiveness; the Oblate and ACC apologies do not.) Asking forgiveness is a controversial element of apology discourse. Whereas a few scholars suggest that an apology ought to be accompanied by a request for forgiveness,[45] many more argue that forgiveness should not be sought.[46] At issue are the power dynamics between the parties and the expectations that may accompany any such request. When forgiveness (or pardon) is sought from God, this invokes and imposes a range of particular theological assumptions on the process, including an understanding of the role of the church in mediating God's forgiveness and pronouncing absolution. When forgiveness, especially in explicitly Christian terms, is sought from human victims, it can impose the expectation that since God forgives the sins of all persons – including victims – then victims ought to forgive as well. This imposition can be damaging for those who have a different spiritual framework or may not be prepared to respond in this way.

The wording of Pope Francis's apologies may serve to control the narrative by defining what the issues are and therefore also what is not on the table. The papal visit reinforced the story that the legacy of the Indian residential schools relates to culture, not to land. Both the Vatican and Maskwacis statements open with praise for Indigenous cultures and values. After celebrating the wisdom of thinking in terms of impacts on the seventh generation, respect for elders, care for lands, and practices of seeking harmony, the pope laments that the residential schools sought to destroy these cultures. A reconciled and repaired state of affairs would be one where the cultures and identities of Indigenous Peoples were respected and valued.[47] Although there is mention of land throughout the statements, it recedes from view as inseparable from Indigenous wisdom. There is no mention of how the land was taken or of the possibility of its restitution. If the problems are defined as individual suffering and loss of culture, acknowledging this suffering and supporting and lauding the recovery of culture appear to be appropriate responses.[48] But if dispossession of the land is the overarching project within which the residential schools were one strategy, a repaired relationship cannot bypass the much more difficult question of land restitution. That means that the wrongdoing did not end with the closing of the last school but remains ongoing.[49]

Pope Francis also minimizes church responsibility by locating the church as also a victim of colonization, a position that appears untenable given the role of the Catholic Church (and other churches) in providing for its ideological foundations, most notably in the Doctrine of Discovery. Although it is fair to say that colonialist attitudes have harmed the church and compromised its mission, the pain of the past for those who are survivors is qualitatively different from the pain of the past for those who represent the perpetrators. Even the very welcome clarification from the Vatican that the Doctrine of Discovery "is not part of the teaching of the Catholic Church" tends to minimize church responsibility for focusing on the canonical status of three particular papal bulls rather than on the broader theological and ecclesiastical culture that enabled and advanced colonialism in a wide variety of ways.[50]

Pope Francis's penitential pilgrimage clearly had moments of risk. Anything that he said or did was fodder for public criticism and rejection. Indeed, the opportunities for Indigenous people to assert agency through a denunciation of the pope's visit, or of the Catholic Church more generally, are important. One noteworthy interruption during the Maskwacis event – the amplified singing in Cree to the tune of the Canadian national anthem by Si Pih Ko – served to reject not only his apology but also his apology story.[51]

Fifth, if a Canadian church's apology for residential schools is an act of recovenanting, the church affirms that some change is required for it to truly be the church that it is called to be. All of the church apologies speak to the need for new relationships between the church (as a primarily settler institution, at least historically, and/or as a body consisting of those who are settlers) and Indigenous people (inside and/or outside of the church). Such relationships are necessarily political since they are about power and about how particular communities are constituted, make decisions, and conduct their affairs. Churches may have identified a range of actions related to "reconciliation" with Indigenous people that may go far beyond the scope of this chapter. Yet the words of apology, the act of apology, and the context surrounding it may each be part of an important microcosm of recovenanting.

All of the church apologies, those from the 1980s and the 1990s and those of Pope Francis, make use of the metaphor of walking together or some variation of journey imagery. This is a powerful image of mutuality, dialogue, solidarity, and common goals. The journey metaphor has the capacity to acknowledge the harmful place where the church has been but also reimagines the nature of the community required to move beyond it. Yet, in addition to the dynamic movement of "walking," there is the image of "together," which is just as significant but also complicated.

According to Peter Bush, when UCC moderator Robert Smith delivered his 1986 apology, he misspoke, asking the Indigenous leader to "walk with us in the Spirit of Christ." To which an elder responded: "'Why do you ask us to walk with you, should we not walk together?'"[52] Although Smith had intended to say "together," the exchange highlighted the challenge that the church faced both in attempting to speak truthfully and penitently about what it had done – that is, what a white Euro-Canadian church had done – and in aspiring to become a church newly constituted by Indigenous people and settlers coming together in some degree of mutuality. When any church speaks to a subset of its members, as the UCC did in speaking to Indigenous members of the UCC, it can ironically highlight the white-settler identity of the church speaking. Changes to the church include the highly symbolic revisions to the UCC crest in 2012 "to acknowledge the presence and spirituality of Indigenous Peoples in the church,"[53] as well as the movement for Indigenous self-determination within the ACC, marked in 2007 by the election of the first national Indigenous bishop.[54]

Several apologies have generated further public statements, including statements with elements of additional apology. The UCC, PCC, and ACC all explicitly built on their apologies in the 1990s in order to make further statements decades later regarding respect for Indigenous spirituality.[55] In the case of the ACC, its 2019 "An Apology for Spiritual Harm" was framed as a supplement to the 1993 apology, addressing a theme that the earlier statement had not adequately addressed. On behalf of the ACC, its primate, Archbishop Fred Hiltz, confessed that it was sinful for the church to have demonized Indigenous spiritualities and to have declared them incompatible with the gospel. He asked Indigenous leaders, "with great respect, to help guide us to honour the wisdom and practice of the past and to live into a truly Indigenous expression of our faith in the future." This text is most explicit about what I refer to here as the recovenanting function of apologies, which seeks to transform past identity for the future.[56]

Although the new statement highlights a gap in the 1993 apology, the fact that such a correction was deemed necessary indicates the abiding significance of apologies as touchstones for the church's collective political life. Apologies can serve as founding documents and as reference points for recovenanting and especially for the work of reconciliation, with the result that, as deficiencies are discerned, they must be amended by new statements. Of course, using apologies in these ways might suggest that they fix attention on words and merely lead to more words. Archbishop Michael Peers himself acknowledged how often his listeners "have heard words which have been empty because they have not been accompanied by actions."[57] Yet many apologies appropriately acknowledge their own inadequacy by noting that they are merely words when what is needed is precisely much more than words.

When the UCC offered its apology in 1986, it was acknowledged but not accepted.[58] That occurred because, according to the Rev. Alf Dumont, an Indigenous UCC elder, an apology "must be lived out if it's to be a real apology."[59] To commemorate the 1986 apology, the UCC constructed a cairn of stones at the site where the apology was offered. But the cairn was deliberately left unfinished. The apology was meant to indicate not resolution or closure but the beginning of something new and open-ended. Events are held there on significant anniversaries of the apology, and stones are to be occasionally added in order to mark important steps on the common journey.[60] This cairn is merely a symbol of a promise of new relationships, yet it also enacts an important aspect of the apology by acknowledging the difficult dialogue and the ongoing work that must be undertaken over time. By publicly locating the apology in place and time, this practice also fosters accountability for the promises made.

Apologies for the Indigenous residential schools are never sufficient, but they may be necessary, as shown by the finally fulfilled call for the pope to apologize. The Canadian church apologies are multifaceted practices through which churches navigate their futures in light of their pasts. They may be deployed in ways that undermine genuine reconciliation. Yet, as political practices with the capacity to acknowledge wrongs, promise action, embody contrition, and hold churches accountable to reorient their identities in transformative ways, such apologies also have the capacity to be important milestones on the journey of truth, justice, and repair.

NOTES

1 Pope Francis, "Angelus," 17 July 2022, https://www.vatican.va/content/francesco/en/angelus/2022/documents/20220717-angelus.html.

2 Truth and Reconciliation Commission of Canada (TRC), *Calls to Action* (2015), https://www2.gov.bc.ca/assets/gov/british-columbians-our-governments/indigenous-people/aboriginal-peoples-documents/calls_to_action_english2.pdf.

3 See Anthony Siegrist, "'Part of the Authority Structure': An Organizational History of Mennonite Indian Residential Schools in Ontario," *Mennonite Quarterly Review* 93, no. 1 (2019): 5–38.

4 Eve Tuck and K. Wayne Yang, "Decolonization Is Not a Metaphor," *Decolonization: Indigeneity, Education and Society* 1, no. 1 (2012): 10.

5 Government of Canada, *Indian Residential Schools Settlement Agreement* (2006), https://www.rcaanc-cirnac.gc.ca/eng/1100100015576/1571581687074.

6 The UCC was formed in 1925 from the union of Methodist, Congregationalist, and some Presbyterian churches. Both the Methodists and Presbyterians ran residential schools, which then became the responsibility of the UCC.

7 The Catholic Church in Canada is structured as dozens of separate legal entities. Schools were run by various religious orders and by several dioceses.

8 For a historical account, see Peter G. Bush, "The Canadian Churches' Apologies for Colonialism and Residential Schools, 1986–1998," *Peace Research* 47, nos 1–2 (2015): 47–70. Although Mennonites also ran schools

and have made some statements of apology, I am limiting my examination to the parties of the *Settlement Agreement.*

9 United Church of Canada, "Apology to Indigenous Peoples," 1986, https://united-church.ca/sites/default/files/apologies-response-crest.pdf. The original title was "Apology to First Nations."

10 Missionary Oblates of Mary Immaculate, "An Apology to the First Nations of Canada," 1991, https://www.cccb.ca/wp-content/uploads/2017/10/oblate_apology_english.pdf.

11 Anglican Church of Canada, "Apology to Native Peoples," 1993, https://www.anglican.ca/tr/apology/english/.

12 Presbyterian Church in Canada, "The Confession of the Presbyterian Church in Canada," 1994, https://presbyterian.ca/downloads/92316/.

13 United Church of Canada, "Apology to Former Students of United Church Indian Residential Schools, and to Their Families and Communities," 1998, https://united-church.ca/sites/default/files/apologies-response-crest.pdf.

14 Canadian Conference of Catholic Bishops, "Letter of the CCCB President to the Indigenous Peoples of Canada," 2018, https://www.cccb.ca/wp-content/uploads/2020/04/4.-Letter_to_Indigenous_Peoples_-_27_March_2018_-_en.pd_.pdf.

15 Christian Paas-Lang, "Papal Apology for Church's Role in Residential Schools May Not Be 'Way Forward': Archbishop," *CBC News*, 6 June 2021, https://www.cbc.ca/news/politics/catholic-church-apology-residential-schools-1.6055303.

16 Bush, "Canadian Churches' Apologies," 60–3.

17 This statement has since been removed from the CCCB website, but it is preserved by the Internet Archive's Wayback Machine. See Canadian Conference of Catholic Bishops, "Catholic Statements of Regret on former Residential Schools," 2020, https://web.archive.org/web/20200426022029/http://www.cccb.ca/site/eng/church-in-canada-and-world/catholic-church-in-canada/indigenous-peoples/3207-catholic-statement-of-regret-on-the-former-residential-schools. A more substantial statement was made the following year. Canadian Conference of Catholic Bishops, "Statement of Apology by the Catholic Bishops of Canada to the Indigen-

ous Peoples of This Land," 24 September 2021, https://www.cccb.ca/letter/statement-of-apology-by-the-catholic-bishops-of-canada-to-the-indigenous-peoples-of-this-land.

18 See the Political Apologies across Cultures database, https://www.politicalapologies.com.

19 Nicholas Tavuchis, *Mea Culpa: A Sociology of Apology and Reconciliation* (Stanford, CA: Stanford University Press, 1991); Aaron Lazare, *On Apology* (New York: Oxford University Press, 2004).

20 See, for example, Elazar Barkan and Alexander Karn, eds, *Taking Wrongs Seriously: Apologies and Reconciliation* (Stanford, CA: Stanford University Press, 2006); Mark Gibney, Rhoda E. Howard-Hassmann, Jean-Marc Coicaud, and Niklaus Steiner, eds, *The Age of Apology: Facing Up to the Past* (Philadelphia: University of Pennsylvania Press, 2008); and Ashraf Rushdy, *A Guilted Age: Apologies for the Past* (Philadelphia: Temple University Press, 2015).

21 In relation to Indian residential school apologies, see Matt James, "Wrestling with the Past: Apologies, Quasi-apologies, and Non-apologies in Canada," in Gibney et al., eds, *Age of Apology*, 137–53; and Sheryl Lightfoot, "Settler-State Apologies to Indigenous Peoples: A Normative Framework and Comparative Assessment," *Native American and Indigenous Studies* 2, no.1 (2015): 15–39.

22 See, for example, Jeff Corntassel and Cindy Holder, "Who's Sorry Now? Government Apologies, Truth Commissions, and Indigenous Self-Determination in Australia, Canada, Guatemala, and Peru," *Human Rights Review* 9, no. 4 (2008): 465–89; Matthew Dorrell, "From Reconciliation to Reconciling: Reading What 'We Now Recognize' in the Government of Canada's 2008 Residential Schools Apology," *English Studies in Canada* 35, no. 1 (2009): 27–45; and Eva Mackey, "The Apologizers' Apology," in *Reconciling Canada: Critical Perspectives on the Culture of Redress*, ed. Jennifer Henderson and Pauline Wakeham, 47–62 (Toronto: University of Toronto Press, 2014). For Harper's apology, see Office of the Prime Minister of Canada, "Indian Residential School Apology," 11 June 2008, https://nctr.ca/exhibits/indian-residential-school-apology/.

23 See, respectively, Janet Bevelas, "An Analysis of Formal Apologies by

Canadian Churches to First Nations" (Centre for Studies in Religion and Society, University of Victoria, 2004); Alain P. Durocher, "Between the Right to Forget and the Duty to Remember: The Politics of Memory in Canada's Public Church Apologies" (PhD diss., Graduate Theological Union, 2002); Neil Funk-Unrau, "Renegotiation of Social Relations through Public Apologies to Canadian Aboriginal Peoples," *Research in Social Movements, Conflicts, and Change* 29 (2008): 1–19; and Bush, "Canadian Churches' Apologies."

24 Jeremy M. Bergen, *Ecclesial Repentance: The Churches Confront Their Sinful Pasts* (London: T&T Clark, 2011).

25 Jeremy M. Bergen, "Whether, and How, a Church Ought to Repent for a Historical Wrong," *Theology Today* 73, no. 2 (2016): 129–48.

26 Chanelle Robinson, "'Papa Don't Preach': Imagining a Theology of Apology in Canada," *Toronto Journal of Theology* 35, no. 1 (2019): 9–24.

27 Alice MacLachlan, "Beyond the Ideal Political Apology," in *On the Uses and Abuses of Political Apologies*, ed. Mihaela Mihai and Mathias Thaler, 13–31 (Basingstoke, UK: Palgrave Macmillan, 2014).

28 MacLachlan, "Beyond the Ideal Political Apology," 22–3.

29 MacLachlan, "Beyond the Ideal Political Apology," 23.

30 Danielle Celermajer, "Apology and the Possibility of the Ethical Nation," in *Public Apology between Ritual and Regret: Symbolic Excuses on False Pretenses or True Reconciliation Out of Sincere Regret?* ed. Daniël Cuypers, Daniel Janssen, Jacques Haers, and Barbara Segaert, 45–64 (Amsterdam: Rodopi, 2013). The religious roots of political apology are developed more thoroughly in Danielle Celermajer, *The Sins of the Nation and the Ritual of Apologies* (Cambridge, UK: Cambridge University Press, 2009).

31 Celermajer, "Apology and the Possibility," 50–4.

32 Celermajer, "Apology and the Possibility," 60.

33 I draw on my detailed analysis of Pope Francis's apologies in Jeremy M. Bergen, "Papal Apologies for Residential Schools and the Stories They Tell," *Journal of Moral Theology* 12, no. 2 (2023): 48–62. See also Jeremy M. Bergen, "Pope Francis's Apology for Residential Schools Doesn't Acknowledge Institutional Responsibility," *The Conversation*, 1 April 2022, https://theconversation.com/pope-franciss-apology-for-residential-

schools-doesnt-acknowledge-institutional-responsibility-180526; and Jeremy M. Bergen, "Pope's Long-Awaited Apology for Indian Residential Schools in Canada Is a 'First Step,'" *The Conversation*, 26 July 2022, https://theconversation.com/popes-long-awaited-apology-for-indian-residential-schools-in-canada-is-a-first-step-187342.

34 See International Theological Commission, *Memory and Reconciliation: The Church and the Faults of the Past* (1999), no. 3.4, https://www.vatican.va/roman_curia/congregations/cfaith/cti_documents/rc_con_cfaith_doc_20000307_memory-reconc-itc_en.html.

35 Pope Francis, "Address of His Holiness Pope Francis: Clementine Hall," 1 April 2022, https://www.vatican.va/content/francesco/en/speeches/2022/april/documents/20220401-popoli-indigeni-canada.html.

36 Pope Francis, "Address of His Holiness: Maskwacis," 25 July 2022, https://www.vatican.va/content/francesco/en/speeches/2022/july/documents/20220725-popolazioniindigene-canada.html.

37 These dynamics are traced and analyzed by Brian P. Flanagan, *Stumbling in Holiness: Sin and Sanctity in the Church* (Collegeville, MN: Liturgical Press, 2018); and Jeanmarie Gribaudo, *A Holy Yet Sinful Church: Three Twentieth-Century Moments in a Developing Theology* (Collegeville, MN: Liturgical Press, 2015). Interestingly, the Oblate apology did not make a strong distinction between the church and its members. Rather, it spoke from the perspective of the order, addressing what "we" did, although perhaps casting the order as a collective of individuals rather than as an ecclesial entity.

38 Pope Francis, "Address of His Holiness Pope Francis: Clementine Hall."

39 Pope Francis, "Address of His Holiness: Maskwacis."

40 United Church of Canada, "Apology to Former Students." Phipps invokes the doctrine of the communion of saints, the Christian belief that all past and present members of the church form a spiritual bond, constituting them as a single community through time.

41 Bush, "Canadian Churches' Apologies," 54.

42 Donna Sinclair, "A Question of Repentance," *United Church Observer*, October 1997, 12–14.

43 See, for example, Raymond J. de Souza, "Should the Pope Apologize …

Again?" *National Post*, 21 December 2015, https://nationalpost.com/opinion/father-raymond-j-de-souza-should-the-pope-apologize-again. Not only did Father Raymond J. de Souza claim that the pope had offered an apology (because Fontaine had called it one), but he also claimed that an apology must be accepted.

44 Pope Francis, "Address of His Holiness Pope Francis: Clementine Hall"; Pope Francis, "Address of His Holiness: Maskwacis."

45 See, for example, Tavuchis, *Mea Culpa*, 22–3.

46 This view is held by the majority in the apology literature. See Thomas Brudholm, "Apology without Forgiveness," *Social Research* 87, no. 4 (2020): 835–61.

47 Pope Francis, "Address of His Holiness: Maskwacis."

48 Referring to Harper's 2008 apology, Eva Mackey names these rhetorical moves as ones that render the offence "apologizeable." Mackey, "Apologizers' Apology," 53–4.

49 In response to the claim in Harper's apology that the Indian residential schools were part of a "sad chapter" now behind us, Glen Sean Coulthard asserts that the colonialism of which the schools were a part enacted an ongoing invasion, and "invasion is a structure not an event." Glen Sean Coulthard, *Red Skin, White Masks: Rejecting the Colonial Politics of Recognition* (Minneapolis: University of Minnesota Press, 2014), 125.

50 Holy See Press Office, "Joint Statement of the Dicasteries for Culture and Education and for Promoting Integral Human Development on the 'Doctrine of Discovery,'" 30 March 2023, para. 6, https://press.vatican.va/content/salastampa/en/bollettino/pubblico/2023/03/30/230330b.html.

51 See Karen Pauls, "'I Couldn't Stay Silent,' Says Cree Singer Who Performed Powerfu Message for Pope Francis," CBC *News*, 29 July 2022, https://www.cbc.ca/news/canada/manitoba/cree-woman-singing-papal-visit-1.6535055.

52 Quoted in Bush, "Canadian Churches' Apologies," 50.

53 United Church of Canada, "Revisions to the United Church of Canada Crest Reflect Inclusion of Indigenous Peoples," 2012, https://united-church.ca/sites/default/files/apologies-response-crest.pdf.

54 On this ongoing process, see Anglican Church of Canada, "Indigenous Ministries," n.d., https://www.anglican.ca/im/ahistory/.

55 United Church of Canada, "Affirming Other Spiritual Paths," 18 February 2015, https://united-church.ca/sites/default/files/affirming-other-spiritual-paths.pdf; Presbyterian Church in Canada, "Statement on Aboriginal Spiritual Practices," 29 January 2015, https://presbyterian.ca/2015/01/29/statement-aboriginal-spiritual-practices/.

56 Anglican Church of Canada, "An Apology for Spiritual Harm," 12 July 2019, https://www.anglican.ca/news/an-apology-for-spiritual-harm/30024511/. The apology concludes by calling on the church to "renew our commitment to our baptismal covenant."

57 Anglican Church of Canada, "Apology to Native Peoples."

58 An official response was given in 1988 by the All Native Circle Conference. In addition to acknowledgment, the response concluded, "In the new spirit this Apology has created, let us unite our hearts and minds in the wholeness of life that the Great Spirit has given us." All Native Circle Conference, "The Response," 1988, https://united-church.ca/sites/default/files/apologies-response-crest.pdf.

59 Quoted in Russell Daye, "An Unresolved Dilemma: Canada's United Church Seeks Reconciliation with Native Peoples," *Ecumenist* 36, no. 2 (1999): 12.

60 See Nancy Devine, "Reflections on an Unfinished Journey: Three People Reflect on the Apology," *Mandate*, May 2005, 3–6; United Church of Canada, "Apology to Action: Reflections on the 35th Anniversary," *YouTube*, 11 June 2021, https://www.youtube.com/watch?v=ZPqMfERAfD8.

7

The Pilgrim Church in Canada

A Penitential People and the 2022 Papal Visit

Niigaanwewidam Sinclair and Darren Dias

We want to walk together, to pray together and to work together, so that the sufferings of the past can lead to a future of justice, healing and reconciliation.

– Pope Francis[1]

PRELUDE TO A PILGRIMAGE

In the wake of the 2006 *Indian Residential Schools Settlement Agreement* and upon the recommendation of the Canadian Conference of Catholic Bishops,[2] Pope Benedict XVI met privately with a small delegation of Indigenous and religious leaders at the Vatican on 29 April 2009. A communiqué following the meeting read that the pope "expressed his sorrow at the anguish caused by the deplorable conduct of some members of the Church and he offered his sympathy and prayerful solidarity."[3] In spite of this visit and the pope's expression of sorrow, sympathy, and prayer, this important gesture did not come close to addressing the immense harm that the Roman Catholic Church perpetrated via Canada's residential school system.

For the entirety of its mandate, the Truth and Reconciliation Commission of Canada (TRC) heard from residential school survivors, Catholics, and clergy that something had to be done to initiate a journey of reconciliation between the church and Indigenous communities. As a result, call 58 of the TRC's *Calls to Action* (2015), part of its multi-volume final report, asked that the church take action:

> We call upon the Pope to issue an apology to Survivors, their families, and communities for the Roman Catholic Church's role in the spiritual, cultural, emotional, physical, and sexual abuse of First Nations, Inuit, and Métis children in Catholic-run residential schools. We call for that apology to be similar to the 2010 apology issued to Irish victims of abuse and to occur within one year of the issuing of this Report and to be delivered by the Pope in Canada.[4]

Unlike the delegation at the 2009 meeting, the TRC asked for a public apology in Canada – to be delivered in front of survivors, their families and communities, and Canadians – for the church's role in residential schools.

Between 28 March and 1 April 2022, a delegation of over 200 First Nations, Inuit, and Métis representatives and their supporters travelled to the Vatican, alongside some Canadian bishops, to be received by Pope Francis. The delegation reiterated call 58 and invited the pope to travel to Canada and to offer an apology – which the pope accepted and committed to do. The purpose of this visit, however, was not just for the delegation to receive this commitment but also for the pope to initiate the first chapter of a symbolic journey. Here, instead of the time-worn stereotype of European discovery – with Christians arriving from European centres to colonize the margins of the so-called New World – Indigenous political and cultural leaders travelled from their centres to another, presenting gifts of diplomacy, relationship, and collective healing.

To get to this place, however, both the Roman Catholic Church and Indigenous leaders would need to navigate some complicated paths. For the Catholic Church, an institution that has accompanied colonizing nations for hundreds of years, this navigation would involve coming to Canada – where the pope and all Catholics would need to face hard truths, recognize the harms perpetrated by Christians, and commit to change and growth. For their part, Indigenous leaders were indeed doing what they had always done by demonstrating to the church what love and partnership look like. This journey to the Vatican, however, would involve travelling into the centres of Catholicism itself as they navigated Bernini's Colonnade, which draws visitors into St Peter's Basilica and into the Apostolic Palace – the centre of the Roman Catholic Church's sacramental and political power and, in Rome, the centre of Christian Europe. Dressed in traditional regalia – clothing that Christians had banned in Canada – the delegation's members entered a room fraught with images of European discovery, yet they were there not to be discovered but to witness the church as it discovered itself, acknowledged what it had done, and heard their call to rebuild relationships.

This process began with an expression of the original language of encounter between Indigenous Peoples and European peoples: the language of gift giving. For Indigenous communities, gifts carry deep symbolism, meaning, and spiritual significance – and the gifts offered to Pope Francis were no different. The Assembly of First Nations gifted a leather stole with orange beaded crosses and a pair of snowshoes; the Métis National Council gave the pope a memory book that included the stories of residential school survivors; and the Inuit delegation offered a baleen cross and sealskin pouch. The gifts not only represented the specific territories, histories, and cultures of each Indigenous group but also stood as invitations to the pope to listen, learn, and share time with the nations that the church had sought to eradicate. In response, the pope gifted Indigenous delegates a bronze olive branch – a symbolic image both from ancient Greece and from the story of Noah's Ark found in the Hebrew Bible. In the Genesis narrative, the olive branch signifies that the flood waters are receding, pointing to the *land* upon which the tree grows – territory where humanity can stand together. The olive branch, in other words, represents the potential for a new relationship between God and creation.

Chief Marie-Anne Day Walker-Pelletier of the Okanese First Nation in Saskatchewan, a survivor of the Lebret Residential School, presented the pope with a pair of moccasins representing the children who did not return home from the residential schools. These moccasins came with an expectation that the pope would return them when he came to Canada to apologize. In many ways, this act would be the first step in this new relationship – a step taken when, on 25 July 2022, Pope Francis returned the moccasins. As the pope said in Maskwacis, "Those moccasins also speak to us of a path to follow."[5]

From 24 to 29 July 2022, Pope Francis made a historic and long-awaited visit to Canada.[6] Both of us – an Indigenous columnist and a priest of the Dominican Order – had participated in the lead-up to the visit in very different ways but met only when we provided television commentary on the visit for the Canadian Broadcasting Corporation. Niigaan Sinclair is a professor of Indigenous studies and a columnist for the *Winnipeg Free Press* who spent years researching Indigenous histories and politics while advocating for the Truth and Reconciliation Commission's *Calls to Action*. Darren Dias is a Dominican priest and professor of theology at the University of St Michael's College at the University of Toronto, where he has done research focused on religious pluralism and Trinitarian theology. He was a part of a collective of Canadian Catholic leaders who wrote a widely disseminated statement calling for a papal apology and for increased church responsibility to Indigenous communities.[7] Both of us, through this work and now friendship, have spent many hours reflecting on the visit.

During his visit to Canada in July 2022, the pope repeatedly referred to his visit as a "penitential pilgrimage," as he had first done in Rome prior to his departure.[8] This chapter uses that concept as the hermeneutic for analyzing the visit by examining the *form* of the visit and by undertaking a critical analysis of the papal discourses. The benefit of this analysis is to ascertain what shape reconciliation may take for Roman Catholic Christians – and perhaps for others too. Although we are aware of many shortcomings of the visit – whether it be dissatisfaction with the text of the apology, the Eucharist celebrated in Edmonton, or the lack of reference to the Doctrine of Discovery, just to mention a few – this chapter is primarily constructive. The remainder is divided into three parts. The next section explores the terms "pilgrimage" and then "penitential." A third section considers themes from the pope's discourses on what he thinks penance – making amends – should reflect. A last section looks beyond the visit itself to some issues that emerged from the pilgrimage. If the pilgrimage began when the Indigenous delegation established a relationship with him through visit and gift exchange, its conclusion is open-ended and future-oriented.

PENITENTIAL PILGRIMAGE

Pilgrimage

Until Pope Paul VI (1963–78), no modern pope had left Rome since 1857.[9] Paul VI made nine pastoral visits to eighteen foreign countries. He often referred to these visits as pilgrimages. For example, upon his arrival in Jordan for his first foreign visit to the Holy Land, the pope described his visit as

> a spiritual one, a humble pilgrimage to the sacred places made holy by the Birth, the Life, the Passion and Death of Jesus Christ, and by His glorious Resurrection and Ascension. At each of these venerable shrines, We shall pray for that peace which Jesus left to His disciples, that peace which the world cannot give.[10]

On his spiritual journey, Pope Paul was to visit specific places sanctified by the life events of Jesus Christ.

Known as the Pilgrim Pope, John Paul II made over one hundred foreign visits, often referring to them as "pilgrimages." For example, the first ever visit of a pope to Nordic countries in 1989 was called an "apostolic pilgrimage." Upon his arrival in Norway he said,

> My pilgrimage to Norway is also in response to the gracious invitation of the *Lutheran Church* to participate in a service of prayer for Christian unity at Nidaros Cathedral, the hallowed national shrine where Saint Olav, King and Martyr, is buried.[11]

The visit to promote ecumenical relations included visiting an important shrine dedicated to a martyr-saint.

The 2009 visit of Pope Benedict XVI (2005–13) to the Holy Land echoed previous understandings of papal pilgrimages as movements toward important commemorative places: "I come to Jordan as a pilgrim, to venerate holy places that have played such an important part in some of the key events of Biblical history."[12] Moreover, upon his arrival in Israel, he said,

> I appreciate the opportunity that has been offered to me to come on pilgrimage to a land that is hallowed by the footsteps of patriarchs and prophets, a land that Christians hold in particular veneration as the setting for the events of the life, death and resurrection of Jesus Christ. I take my place in a long line of Christian pilgrims to these shores.[13]

These papal speeches reflect a fairly common understanding of pilgrimage: the movement of a pilgrim to a specific destination, space, or place considered sacred because it has been made holy by the life events of a figure of historical and spiritual significance.

Somewhat differently, Pope Francis's penitential pilgrimage in 2022 included visits to sites where children had suffered and died, to sites where political policy had aligned with ideas about the religious deliverance of Indigenous people, and to other places of significance to Canadian Catholics. Moreover, these sites were generally not locations made significant primarily by a singular historical or spiritual figure. On his visit to Canada, during his stop at the pilgrimage site of Lac Ste Anne on 26 July 2022, Pope Francis referred to the more traditional understanding of pilgrimage as a movement toward a holy place: "Here we can truly feel the choral heartbeat of a pilgrim people, of generations who set out on a journey towards the Lord in order to experience his work of healing."[14] Here, the site is holy not because it was visited by a paradigmatic Christian figure but because of the significance that it had for Indigenous Peoples long before European settlement. Further, the site is sanctified by its natural waters and their potential to heal. Drawing from the Hebrew Bible, Pope Francis links water to healing:

> Dear brothers and sisters, pilgrims to these waters, the word of God can help us realize what we can draw from them. The prophet Ezekiel tells us twice that the waters flowing [from] the Temple both "give life" and "heal" God's people (cf. *Ezek* 47: 8–9).[15]

It is hard not to see this gesture as an olive branch to Indigenous cultures and communities that similarly hold a deep respect and reverence for water to "give life" and "heal" too.

On 25 July, Pope Francis travelled to Maskwacis in order to deliver the long-overdue apology on behalf of the Roman Catholic Church. Here, he sums up the intent of his pilgrimage: "We want to walk together, to pray together and to work together, so that the sufferings of the past can lead to a future of justice, healing and reconciliation." He also speaks for the first time in Canada about his visit as a "penitential pilgrimage":

> I have been waiting to come here and be with you! Here, from this place associated with painful memories, I would like to begin what I consider a pilgrimage, a penitential pilgrimage. I have come to your native lands to tell you in person of my sorrow, to implore God's forgiveness, healing and reconciliation, to express my closeness and to pray with you and for you.[16]

Aside from a reference to "native lands," there is no trace of a movement toward a specific place or shrine in Pope Francis's pilgrimage. Instead, he says, "This pilgrimage is taking place over several days and in places far distant from one another." According to this expansive notion, pilgrimage is not limited to a specific place or time since it is bounded only by a "future of justice, healing and reconciliation."[17]

In Pope Francis's understanding of pilgrimage, which extends beyond a view of pilgrimage as centred on a significant place, the journey itself brings about "the possibility of creating social and/or psychological transformation" by escaping everyday life and subverting established boundaries.[18] For Pope Francis, the pilgrimage to Canada for apology reflects the reframing of pilgrimage proposed by Simon Coleman and John Eade, a reframing that centres pilgrimage less on place and more on motion and movement. They enumerate four distinct but interrelated understandings of pilgrimage that assist in an analysis of the pope's pilgrimage to Canada. First, pilgrimage is "movement as performative action." Pope Francis's movement is from the centre to the periphery. This direction refers to the possibility of social and cultural transformation in the performance of pilgrimage that subverts the centre-periphery relationship. Second, this movement is an "embodied action." This apology takes place in face-to-face encounters conducted on the ground where the abuse happened. Next, movement is part of a semantic field. Therefore, as Coleman and Eade explain, it is necessary to "to contextualize the meaning of 'pilgrimage' within the local understandings of mobility … or such terms as space, place and landscape."[19] Last, they refer to movement as "metaphor" to capture the fact that pilgrimages may "evoke movement rather than require its physical instantiation."[20] In this sense, Pope Francis invokes not just the movement of the pope but also the movement of all those in communion with the bishop of Rome and with the Roman Catholic Church in Canada as they walk with Indigenous communities on a path of reconciliation. Enacted beyond the visit's physical instantiation in space and time, beyond even the movements and actions of the visit itself, these movements are unfinished.

Geographical Metaphor

The penitential pilgrimage can be divided into three legs. The first leg of the pilgrimage took place in Alberta, the province that had the most residential schools. At Maskwacis, Pope Francis made a formal apology for the Catholic Church's involvement in residential schools, after which he met with Indigenous Catholics at Sacred Heart Church of the First

Peoples. The next day, the pope presided over Eucharist in Edmonton and made a pilgrimage to Lac Ste Anne. The second leg of the journey was from 27 to 28 July in Quebec. It began with a meeting with political leaders at the Citadelle de Québec. The following day, the pope celebrated Mass at the National Shrine of Ste-Anne-de-Beaupre and then met with religious leaders at the Cathedral-Basilica of Notre-Dame de Québec, seat of the first Roman Catholic diocese in North America. On 29 July, after meeting with some delegations, the pope travelled to Iqaluit for the last leg of his visit. While there, he met privately with former residential school students before a public event involving the youth.

The first leg of the pilgrimage in Alberta focused on the past, the fact of the residential schools, the suffering that this system caused, and the involvement of the Catholic Church in this colonial system. It took place on the land of those who had witnessed generations of violence – the very land whose natural resources had been impetuses for the colonial project. The movement from Maskwacis, which represented the place of suffering, to the local Indigenous Catholic community and then to the pilgrim waters of Lac Ste Anne was a movement toward healing. The second leg of the journey took place in Quebec City, the first European colony in North America, centre of the French Administration, and site of the British Conquest on the Plains of Abraham. As much as Quebec was a political centre, it was also the religious centre of the Roman Catholic Church in Canada and home to the first diocese in Canada, which sent missionaries to the West. The events on this leg of the pilgrimage took place at the Citadelle de Québec (secular power) and at the Roman Catholic cathedral (religious power). Here, Pope Francis was surrounded by religious leaders (i.e., bishops, priests, religious, and pastoral workers) and political elite (i.e., heads of state and government). This leg of the pilgrimage focused on the present situation of Indigenous communities and their relationship with Christians and Canadians today. It recognized the lasting effects of residential schools and the multi-generational trauma suffered by Indigenous communities. In his speeches, the pope called for renewed relationships to benefit the common good.

From this historic centre of power, Pope Francis went to Iqaluit in Canada's northern territory, where he spoke to survivors and then to the youth. The last event of the pilgrimage took place in a youth centre and involved the youth as representatives of the future. In addressing the youth of Iqaluit, Pope Francis ended his pilgrimage by saying,

> You were made to soar upwards, towards the most genuine, true and beautiful desires that you cherish in your hearts, to love God and to serve your neighbour. Don't think that life's great dreams are as unattainable as the sky above … So never lose hope, fight, give it your all, and you will not be sorry. Go forward on your journey, "step by step towards the best."[21]

The pilgrimage began by bearing witness to suffering in Maskwacis, moved to the centre of colonial political and religious power in Quebec, and concluded in Iqaluit by invoking the future possibilities to be found in Indigenous cultures and communities – classically framed at the margin/periphery of the country. This reframing recentres the political and spiritual foundation of Canada in its original peoples and directs Catholics to learn from these original peoples while forging a path to the future. The dynamic relationship between the periphery/margin and the centre was reflected in Pope Francis's thought. For him, those on the periphery/margin challenge the hegemonic regimes of the powerful, who take what should be at the disposal of all for the common good and centre it on themselves and their benefit. Those on the periphery/margin unmask the truth of ideologies that serve the interests of the powerful. In Pope Francis's view, those on the periphery/margin must be invited and perhaps drawn into the centre if they are to actively participate in the construction of society.[22] Indeed, the centre should be repositioned to include other centres too. Doing so blurs the line between centre and periphery by regarding the margins not as places of powerlessness but as dynamic places of creativity, tenacity, faithfulness, strategy, and diversity.

Penitential Dimensions

Pope Francis began the long-awaited apology by saying that it was but the "first step" on his "penitential pilgrimage":

> I am here because the first step of my penitential pilgrimage among you is that of again asking forgiveness, of telling you once more that I am deeply sorry. Sorry for the ways in which, regrettably, many Christians supported the colonizing mentality of the powers that oppressed the indigenous peoples. I am sorry. I ask forgiveness, in particular, for the ways in which many members of the Church and of religious communities cooperated, not least through their indifference, in projects of cultural destruction and forced assimilation promoted by the governments of that time, which culminated in the system of residential schools.[23]

Later that day, at Sacred Heart Church of the First Peoples, the pope repeated that he was only beginning a pilgrimage that had to do with expressing sorrow and seeking forgiveness: "I wanted to make this penitential pilgrimage, which I began this morning by recalling the wrong done to the indigenous peoples by many Christians and by asking with sorrow for forgiveness."[24]

It is critical to understand, however, that this "first step" was not *actually* the first step of the 2022 visit – for the journey of the visit had already started months before at the Vatican, years before with the work of the TRC, and decades before through lobbying for papal attention and apologies. Pope Francis was very careful with his language, here framing the visit not as a singular action that embodied reconciliation but as a model for how he understood and imagined reconciliation taking place for Catholics. A "penitential pilgrimage," beginning with his arrival in Canada to deliver an apology, was thus how he believed Catholics needed to proceed in order to build and to repair relations with Indigenous communities.

As discussed previously, one way of understanding this pilgrimage is in terms of how it illustrates a reframing of the country that relocates its traditional centres of power at the margins. But the modifier "penitential" determines the character of this movement, one familiar in Catholic sacramental theology. Penitential pilgrimages are not new to the Christian tradition. Medieval penitential practices often required serious sinners to make a public confession and then a pilgrimage to a holy site or a monastery. These practices were developments within the history of one of the Roman Catholic Church's seven sacraments, known as the sacrament of penance or, synonymously, as the sacrament of confession or reconciliation. Four distinct moments constitute the sacrament: contrition, confession, penance, and absolution. Contrition, the authentic feeling of sorrow for the sin committed, moves the penitent to auricular confession. Pope Francis refers to the sorrow that he felt during his encounter with the Indigenous delegation that had come to the Vatican in April of that year to invite him to Canada. Authentic contrition makes the confession of sin possible. Articulating the wrongs committed through an expression of sorrow refers to the reality of a situation and can be humbling and shameful for the penitent. But more importantly, it confirms the wrongs that were suffered by the other and affirms the truth of the situation. The third moment is penance, which entails making satisfaction or amends for the wrongdoings and committing oneself to not repeating the sins. Because of contrition, confession, and penance (or making amends), absolution is possible. A penitential pilgrimage must therefore be understood not merely as an expression of sorrow and regret (or contrition). It does not end in the articulation of wrongdoing in an apology but must also include penance and the making of amends for wrongs committed as it moves to recentre the other in seeking the forgiveness and absolution needed to forge a different and renewed relationship.

Pope Francis's penitential pilgrimage represented a movement both geographically from the centre to the peripheries and relationally toward the other. If Pope Francis had expressed only contrition and confessed the sin of the church in his apology, some might have appreciated his words, but the apology would have been neither a demonstration of action nor an illustration of what the church must do in the performance of contrition, confession, and penance for the many wrongs that it committed. Making amends includes realizing the TRC's call to action, meeting agreed-upon financial obligations, and listening to Indigenous voices and following their lead, but Francis also opened up some themes for the Catholic Church to reflect upon in its efforts at reconciliation. The next section enumerates several of these themes drawn from Pope Francis's various discourses.

THEMES OF MAKING AMENDS IN POPE FRANCIS'S SPEECHES

The Face of God in the Other

In his address to ecclesial leaders at the Cathedral-Basilica of Notre-Dame de Québec, Pope Francis queried how the church could bear witness to its claims about Jesus Christ in spite of ideological rifts and disunity within the church. Drawing from his encyclical *Fratelli Tutti*,[25] the pope speaks of the church as a "Christian community that in this way becomes a school of humanity, where all can learn to love one another as brothers and sisters, ready to work together for the common good."[26] When the Christian community loves others, it becomes a school of humanity, a witness to human solidarity and the common good. The call to build human community is rooted in the anthropological claim that God's presence is reflected in all of God's children. The pope says,

> This is the way: to build relationships of fraternity with everyone, with indigenous brothers and sisters, with every sister and brother we meet, *because the presence of God is reflected in each of their faces.*[27]

If God's presence is reflected in each of their faces, there can be no doubt that God is present with all humans, as well as in their cultures and traditions, independent of Western culture and the Judeo-Christian dispensation.

Perhaps this statement is one of the most significant that the pope made, a statement that lies at the heart of a renewed relationship between (settler) Christians and Indigenous Peoples: the affirmation of a common and full humanity because of the presence of God that dwells within every human person. This statement made in Quebec while addressing ecclesial leaders answers the sixteenth-century question that gave rise to the Valladolid debates.

Between 1550 and 1551, the Catholic Church heard a debate between the Dominican Bartolome de las Casas and Juan Gines de Sepulveda in Valladolid, Spain, regarding the ethics surrounding the forceful and bloody conquest of the Americas and what to do with the Indigenous Peoples there. In essence, the debate was whether Indigenous Peoples of the Americas were humans and, thus, were redeemable by Christ. Sepulveda's position was simple. Citing previous papal bulls claiming that non-Christians had no rights and were suitable only for slavery, he claimed that Indigenous Peoples were absent of reason and God and deserved no regard. In response, and arguing for their intellectual and religious capacity, de las Casas posited that Indigenous Peoples simply needed to hear the word of God and to experience peaceful and persuasive conversion. In the end, church leaders made no conclusions, except to agree that the conversion of Indigenous Peoples should be attempted.

In Quebec City, Pope Francis answered this nearly five-hundred-year-old debate with finality: not only are Indigenous Peoples human, but in their own cultures, languages, dress, and civilizations, the "presence of God is reflected in each of their faces." Conversion of Indigenous Peoples is, simply put, redundant – rendering the conquest of the Americas, longstanding Christian notions of Indigenous inferiority, and the entire project of residential schools in Canada a misguided misunderstanding of God's will.

Memory

In his apology to Indigenous Peoples for the Roman Catholic Church's involvement in residential schools, Pope Francis connected memory and land to forgetfulness and indifference. "These are lands that speak to us; they enable us to *remember*."[28] In the face of assimilationist policies that aim at erasing memory, the land does not forget as it bears witness to the violent colonial appropriation and extraction of the land, its resources, and its peoples. For Pope Francis, not remembering leads dangerously to indifference:

> Yet it is right to remember, because forgetfulness leads to indifference and, as has been said, "the opposite of love is not hatred, it's indifference … and the opposite of life is not death, it's indifference" … To remember the devastating experiences that took place in the residential schools hurts, angers, causes pain, and yet it is necessary.[29]

Francis quotes Shoah survivor Elie Wiesel, whose reflections are foundational in genocide studies. Wiesel equates indifference with a form of hatred that he calls "the opposite of love." The monition around indifference is addressed not only to settlers whose indifference permitted the abuses in the schools to take place historically but also to contemporary Canadians who are indifferent to the injustices experienced by Indigenous communities that continue to this day as a result of ongoing colonization.

Simply put, the Catholic Church cannot preach indifference when it comes to institutional actions, and Catholics must not be indifferent to a church that performs actions in their names. Catholics must be engaged, ask questions, and bear witness to the institution for it to be a church of Catholics. If violently taking land and forcibly removing peoples from their lands is at the heart of the colonial project that resulted in the residential school system, then remembering the place of land in reconciliation and not remaining indifferent to others are central to making amends.

Creation

Two tropes found in Pope Francis's discourses throughout the visit are also found elsewhere in his teachings, particularly in his encyclical *Laudato Si'* (2015) and in his post-synodal reflection *Querida Amazonia* (2020):[30] human relationship with creation and ongoing forms of colonization.

The pope draws attention to the fact that Western settler relations with the earth, which can be characterized as exploitative and extractivist,[31] stand in contrast to the wisdom of Indigenous ways of relating to the earth and in contrast to the deep relationship of the earth to life itself:

> Here, immersed in creation, we can also sense another beating: the maternal heartbeat of the earth. Just as the hearts of babies in the womb beat in harmony with those of their mothers, so in order to grow as people, we need to harmonize our own rhythms of life with those of creation, which gives us life.[32]

The alienation from the land and its exploitation that characterize Western settler cultures and economies are contrasted by Pope Francis with what can be learned from Indigenous knowledge and wisdom:

> The native peoples extracted maple sap, with which they concocted wholesome and healthy syrups. This makes us think of their industriousness and their constant concern to protect the land and the environment, in fidelity to a harmonious vision of creation as an open book that teaches human beings to love the Creator and to live in symbiosis with other living creatures. We can learn much from this ability to listen attentively to God, to persons and to nature.[33]

Indigenous wisdom and knowledge provide alternative ways of relating to the earth, ways that promote integrity and healing. In theological language, Francis says that these ways of relating can inculcate love not only for fellow creatures but also for the Creator.

Rethinking settler relationships with the land via capitalism, competitiveness, and individuality and all that these values promote and sustain is a central part of the reconciliation process. Indigenous nations and values of community, reciprocity, and collectivity are models for new ways of living in right relationship with the church, with the earth and water, and with God.

Colonization

Any consideration of relations with the land must reflect on colonization. Unfortunately, Pope Francis speaks less specifically about decolonization and the land and more about ongoing forms of colonization. In speaking about ongoing forms of colonization, the pope does not speak specifically to the Canadian context but is more concerned with the reality of global, neoliberal, capitalist ideological colonization – a form of colonization that is also at the centre of Canada's extractivist land settlement policies. In addressing political leaders at the Citadelle de Québec, located in the colonial capital of the French regime, the pope says,

> That "history of suffering and contempt," the fruit of the colonizing mentality, "does not heal easily." Indeed, it should make us realize that "colonization has not ended; in many places it has been transformed, disguised and concealed" … This is the case with forms of ideological colonization. In the past, the colonialist mentality disregarded the concrete life of people and imposed certain predetermined cultural models; yet today too, there are any number of forms of ideological colonization that clash with the reality of life, stifle the natural attachment of peoples to their values, and attempt to uproot their traditions, history and religious ties.[34]

Pope Francis laments that the ideological colonization of today looks only to immediate satisfactions, is intolerant of difference, and neglects the duty of care for the most vulnerable and marginalized, who suffer "amid general indifference."[35]

Indigenous Traditions

On the last stop of his penitential pilgrimage, Pope Francis addressed both the elders and the youth of Iqaluit. If the first leg of the journey looked to the past and the second leg commented on the present, Pope Francis was decidedly future-oriented in his discourses in Iqaluit. He offered words of perseverance, affirmation, and hope to the youth based on the resilience of the survivors he encountered earlier in the day. Referencing the biblical story of Naboth, the pope praised those who refused to give their inheritance to those in power: "Those forced assimilations evoke another biblical story, that of the just man Naboth (cf. *1 Kings* 21), who refused to give the vineyard he had inherited from his ancestors to those in power, who were willing to use every means to snatch it from him."[36] After centuries of assimilationist policies, encouraged and sustained by Christian missionaries, Pope Francis praised Indigenous people who had resisted these polices, often at great personal expense. Because of the perseverance of the elders, Pope Francis could say to the youth, "That is what you are, a perennial testimony to the life that never ends, a light that shines and that no one has been able to extinguish."[37] The perseverance and resilience of previous generations bear witness to life in the face of a culture of death.

The pope goes on to name some of the values that have been handed down, emphasizing again care for others and the environment:

> You have come to love these places, to respect, cherish and enhance them, passing on, from generation to generation, such basic values as respect for the elderly, genuine fraternity and care for the environment. There is a beautiful and harmonious relationship between you and this land you inhabit, because it too is strong and resilient.[38]

He then challenges the youth to remember:

> Caring, teaching and learning how to care: to this task young people in particular, supported by the example of their elders, have been called! Care for the earth, care for your people, care for your history.[39]

Just as Pope Francis began his discourses in Canada with a clarion call to remember in the face of indifference, he concludes his visit by encouraging the youth to remember the very traditions that were suppressed by settlers and missionaries and have survived because of the resilience and commitment of elders.

Action

On the first day of his penitential pilgrimage, Pope Francis recalled his initial meeting with the Indigenous delegation: "In Rome, after I listened to your stories, I stated that 'any truly effective process of healing requires concrete actions.'"[40] The pope, who greatly appreciated symbolic gestures, was aware of the empty promises and hollow words that had characterized recent attempts at reconciliation and that rightly complicated the present work of reconciliation. Although in this address he does not offer a concrete plan of action, he does commit the local churches to figuring one out:

> Dear brothers and sisters: gestures and visits can be important, but most words and deeds of reconciliation take place at the local level, in communities like this, where individuals and families travel side-by-side, day by day. To pray together, to help one another, to share life stories, common joys and common struggles: this is what opens the door to the reconciling work of God.[41]

Pope Francis commits the Catholic Church in Canada to the path of reconciliation not only at the level of policy but also in local communities and in people's everyday lives.

AFTER THE PILGRIMAGE

As became common in the papacy of Pope Francis, his conversation with media people on the flight back to Rome proved significant. Questions from members of the media amplified two significant concerns that had arisen during the penitential pilgrimage to Canada but had not been directly addressed by the pope while he was there. The first was the naming of the assimilationist policies and practices of the Canadian state and the churches as "genocide." The second related to repealing the Doctrine of Discovery.

Genocide

Anishinaabe journalist Brittany Hobson of the Canadian Press asked whether Pope Francis agreed that members of the church had participated in genocide, reminding him that the TRC had changed its language from "cultural genocide" to simply "genocide." In his response, the pope gave examples of only cultural genocide, commenting on the wrongs of "taking away children, changing culture, changing mentality, changing traditions, changing a race, let's put it that way, an entire culture," but he concluded, "Yes, genocide is a technical word. I didn't use it because it didn't come to my mind, but I described it … Yes, it's genocide."[42] The pope referred to the technical nature of the term "genocide." The United Nations' definition of genocide is "a crime committed with the intent to destroy a national, ethnic, racial or religious group, in whole or in part."[43] Three months after the pope's affirmation of the residential school system as genocide, the Canadian House of Commons also recognized the residential school system as an act of genocide. The same motion that had failed in June 2021.[44]

Doctrine of Discovery

On 25 July 2022, following Pope Francis's apology at Maskwacis in an emotionally charged atmosphere, Chief Judy Wilson of the Neskonlith First Nation yelled, "Repudiate the doctrine of discovery! Renounce the papal bulls!"[45] This call was to become a chorus for the rest of the visit and beyond. The Doctrine of Discovery is a series of papal bulls giving European invaders "the license to claim vacant land (*terra nullius*)" – that is, land not inhabited by Christians – and giving European powers and their nation-state successors "sovereignty, dominion, title and jurisdiction."[46] The doctrine was based primarily on Pope Nicholas V's bull *Inter*

Caetera (1493). In 2010, the Vatican made clear at the United Nations that the bull had already been abrogated by the *Treaty of Tordesillas* (1494), *Sublimus Deus* (1537), and *Immensa Pastorum* (1741), by numerous papal encyclicals, and by canon 6 of the current *Code of Canon Law*. Further, circumstances were such that the doctrine was without "legal or doctrinal value."[47] On the plane ride home from his pilgrimage to Canada, Pope Francis was asked about the repudiation of the doctrine of discovery. He did not seem to appreciate the importance of the doctrine and seemed to equate it with colonial policies and practices. However, on 30 March 2023, a joint statement from the Dicastery for Culture and Education and the Dicastery for Promoting Integral Human Development stated, "The Catholic Church therefore repudiates those concepts that fail to recognize the inherent human rights of indigenous peoples, including what has become known as the legal and political 'doctrine of discovery.'"[48] Technically, the statement does not repudiate the doctrines themselves but the "concepts" behind them that deny Indigenous rights. Nonetheless, the doctrines are considered abrogated and not in force theologically, although they are still relied upon in law.

CONCLUSION

Unlike Pope Benedict XVI's 2009 statement of "sorrow,"[49] Pope Francis's July 2022 penitential pilgrimage illustrated "movement as performative action,"[50] gifting the church a method of movement from the centre to the periphery and a model of social and cultural transformation. Through "embodied action,"[51] Pope Francis invoked not just a movement of the pope but also a movement of all Catholics in Canada as they walk meaningfully together, shaped by the land, and in a new relationship with Indigenous communities.[52] Although hardly perfect, this journey fulfilled much of the TRC's call 58 and embodied a path for Catholics in Canada to achieve healing and to move toward penance and – perhaps one day – reconciliation.

NOTES

1 Pope Francis, "Address of His Holiness: Maskwacis," 25 July 2022, https://www.vatican.va/content/francesco/en/speeches/2022/july/documents/20220725-popolazioniindigene-canada.html.

2 Government of Canada, *Indian Residential Schools Settlement Agreement* (2006), https://www.rcaanc-cirnac.gc.ca/eng/1100100015576/1571581687074.

3 Vatican, "Canada: Communiqué of the Holy See Press Office," 29 April 2009, https://www.vatican.va/resources/resources_canada-first-nations-apr2009_en.html. See also Canadian Conference of Catholic Bishops, "Pope Benedict XVI Meets with Representatives of Former Indian Residential School Students and the Church in Canada," n.d. https://www.cccb.ca/indigenous-peoples/resources/indian-residential-schools-truth-reconciliation-commission/pope-benedict-xvi.

4 Truth and Reconciliation Commission of Canada (TRC), *Calls to Action* (2015), https://www2.gov.bc.ca/assets/gov/british-columbians-our-governments/indigenous-people/aboriginal-peoples-documents/calls_to action_english2.pdf.

5 Pope Francis, "Address of His Holiness: Maskwacis."

6 Vatican, "Apostolic Journey of His Holiness Pope Francis to Canada, 24–30 July 2022," 23 June 2022, https://www.vatican.va/content/francesco/en/travels/2022/outside/documents/canada-2022.html.

7 "Statement from Concerned Canadian Catholics on the Discoveries in Kamloops," *Change.org*, n.d., https://www.change.org/p/canadian-conference-of-catholic-bishops-statement-from-concerned-canadian-catholics-on-the-discoveries-in-kamloops-fdaf3705-463e-4bac-9354-b8203a4762a6.

8 Pope Francis, "Angelus," 17 July 2022, https://www.vatican.va/content/francesco/en/angelus/2022/documents/20220717-angelus.html.

9 Pope John XXIII did visit Assisi once in 1962.

10 Pope Paul VI, "Address to the King of Jordan," 4 January 1964, https://www.vatican.va/content/paul-vi/en/speeches/1964/documents/hf_p-vi_spe_19640104_jordania.html.

11 John Paul II, "Address of His Holiness: Fornebu International Airport, Oslo," 1 June 1989, original emphasis, https://www.vatican.va/content/john-paul-ii/en/speeches/1989/june/documents/hf_jp-ii_spe_19890601_arrivo-norvegia.html.

12 Pope Benedict XVI, "Address of His Holiness: 'Queen Alia' International Airport of Amman," 8 May 2009, https://www.vatican.va/content/benedict-xvi/en/speeches/2009/may/documents/hf_ben-xvi_spe_20090508_welcome-amman.html.

13 Pope Benedict XVI, "Address of His Holiness: 'Ben Gurion' International Airport – Tel Aviv," 11 May 2009, https://www.vatican.va/content/benedict-xvi/en/speeches/2009/may/documents/hf_ben-xvi_spe_20090511_welcome-tel-aviv.html.

14 Pope Francis, "Homily of the Holy Father: Lac Ste. Anne," 26 July 2022, https://www.vatican.va/content/francesco/en/homilies/2022/documents/20220726-omelia-lacsteanne-canada.html.

15 Pope Francis, "Homily of the Holy Father: Lac Ste. Anne."

16 Pope Francis, "Address of His Holiness: Maskwacis."

17 Pope Francis, "Address of His Holiness: Maskwacis."

18 Simon Coleman and John Eade, "Introduction: Reframing Pilgrimage," in *Reframing Pilgrimage: Cultures in Motion*, ed. Simon Coleman and John Eade (London: Routledge, 2004), 2.

19 Coleman and Eade, "Introduction," 16.

20 Coleman and Eade, "Introduction," 17.

21 Pope Francis, "Address of His Holiness: Primary School in Iqaluit," 29 July 2022, https://www.vatican.va/content/francesco/en/speeches/2022/july/documents/20220729-giovani-anziani-iqaluit.html.

22 See Darren Dias, "Paulo Freire and Pope Francis on Dialogue: An Anticolonial Interpretation," *Espacio, Tiempo y Educacion* 9, no. 1 (2022): 83–98.

23 Pope Francis, "Address of His Holiness: Maskwacis."

24 Pope Francis, "Address of His Holiness: Sacred Heart Church at Edmonton," 25 July 2022, https://www.vatican.va/content/francesco/en/speeches/2022/july/documents/20220725-incontroedmonton-canada.html.

25 Pope Francis, *Fratelli Tutti*, 3 October 2020, https://www.vatican.va/content/francesco/en/encyclicals/documents/papa-francesco_20201003_enciclica-fratelli-tutti.html.

26 Pope Francis, "Homily of His Holiness: Basilica of Notre-Dame de Quebec," 28 July 2022, https://www.vatican.va/content/francesco/en/homilies/2022/documents/20220728-omelia-vespri-quebec.html.

27 Pope Francis, "Homily of His Holiness: Basilica," emphasis added.

28 Pope Francis, "Address of His Holiness: Maskwacis," original emphasis.

29 Pope Francis, "Address of His Holiness: Maskwacis," quoting Elie Wiesel, interviewed in Alvin P. Sanoff, "One Must Not Forget," *U.S. News and World Report* (Washington, DC), 27 October 1986.

30 Pope Francis, *Laudato Si'*, 24 May 2015, https://www.vatican.va/content/francesco/es/encyclicals/documents/papa-francesco_20150524_enciclica-laudato-si.html; Pope Francis, *Querida Amazonia*, 2 February 2020, https://www.vatican.va/content/francesco/en/apost_exhortations/documents/papa-francesco_esortazione-ap_20200202_querida-amazonia.html. See also Bradford Hinze, "Dreams of Synodality, Specters of Constraint," *Louvain Studies* 43, no. 3 (2020): 297–312.

31 Pope Francis states, "They can inspire us all, and help to heal harmful tendencies to exploitation. Exploiting creation, relationships, time and basing human activity solely on what proves useful and profitable." Pope Francis, "Address of His Holiness: Citadelle de Québec," 27 July 2022, https://www.vatican.va/content/francesco/en/speeches/2022/july/documents/20220727-autorita-canada.html.

32 Pope Francis, "Homily of the Holy Father: Lac Ste. Anne."

33 Pope Francis, "Address of His Holiness: Citadelle de Québec."

34 Pope Francis, "Address of His Holiness: Citadelle de Québec," quoting Pope Francis, *Querida Amazonia*, para. 16.

35 Pope Francis, "Address of His Holiness: Citadelle de Québec."

36 Pope Francis, "Address of His Holiness: Primary School in Iqaluit."

37 Pope Francis, "Address of His Holiness: Primary School in Iqaluit."

38 Pope Francis, "Address of His Holiness: Primary School in Iqaluit."

39 Pope Francis, "Address of His Holiness: Primary School in Iqaluit."

40 Pope Francis, "Address of His Holiness: Sacred Heart Church," quoting Pope Francis, "Address of His Holiness Pope Francis: Clementine Hall," 1 April 2022, https://www.vatican.va/content/francesco/en/speeches/2022/april/documents/20220401-popoli-indigeni-canada.html.

41 Pope Francis, "Address of His Holiness: Sacred Heart Church."

42 Pope Francis, "Press Conference on the Return Flight to Rome," 29 July 2022, https://www.vatican.va/content/francesco/en/speeches/2022/july/documents/20220729-voloritorno-canada.html. See also Richard Raycraft, "MPs Back Motion Calling on Government to Recognize Residential Schools Program as Genocide," *CBC News*, 27 October 2022, https://www.cbc.ca/news/politics/house-motion-recognize-genocide-1.6632450.

43 United Nations, *Convention on the Prevention and Punishment of the Crime of Genocide* (1948), https://www.un.org/en/genocideprevention/documents/Genocide%20Convention-FactSheet-ENG.pdf.

44 Andrea Sakiyama Kennedy, "House of Commons Recognizes Residential Schools as a Genocide," *Nunatsiaq News*, 28 October 2022, https://nunatsiaq.com/stories/article/house-of-commons-recognizes-residential-schools-as-genocide/.

45 Quoted in Anna Mehler Paperny, "Pope's Apology in Canada Falls Short for Some Indigenous Survivors," *Reuters*, 27 July 2022, https://www.reuters.com/world/americas/popes-apology-canada-falls-short-some-indigenous-survivors-2022-07-27/.

46 Indigenous Corporate Training, "Indigenous Title and the Doctrine of Discovery, 30 March 2023, https://www.ictinc.ca/blog/indigenous-title-and-the-doctrine-of-discovery.

47 "Statement by Permanent Observer Mission of the Holy See," presented to the Economic and Social Council, 9th Session of the Permanent Forum on Indigenous Issues, New York, 27 April 2010, https://www.cccb.ca/wp-content/uploads/2020/01/Holy-See.pdf.

48 Holy See Press Office, "Joint Statement of the Dicasteries for Culture and Education and for Promoting Integral Human Development on the 'Doctrine of Discovery,'" 30 March 2023, para. 7, https://press.vatican.va/content/salastampa/it/bollettino/pubblico/2023/03/30/0238/00515.html.

49 Vatican, "Canada: Communiqué of the Holy See Press Office."

50 Coleman and Eade, "Introduction," 16.

51 Coleman and Eade, "Introduction," 16.

52 On pilgrimage and journey, see Raymond C. Aldred and Matthew R. Anderson, *Our Home and Treaty Land* (Altona, MB: Friesen, 2024), 2–5.

Epilogue

Doris M. Kieser and Jane Barter

On 21 April 2025, Easter Monday, mere months after the completion of this collection, Pope Francis died. It is fitting that a pope committed to hope, inclusion, and encounter died over the Feast of the Resurrection of Christ. He was eighty-eight years old, and his health had declined in his final years. He had, however, outlived his own prediction for a short pontificate of two to three years.

In his twelve years in St Peter's Chair, Pope Francis stood squarely with marginalized and oppressed people across the globe. It is therefore no surprise that in 2022 he had undertaken what he called his "penitential pilgrimage,"[1] whose motto was "Walking Together," to apologize and repent for the Catholic Church's role in the colonization and abuse of Indigenous Peoples in Canada. Although it is too soon to assess the overall legacy of Pope Francis's papacy, we might well address some of the proximate results of his apologies to First Nations, Inuit, and Métis people in Canada. The ultimate assessment of this visit lies within the experiences of each individual person for whom this visit was important, most significantly survivors of Indian residential schools, their families, and their communities.

Was it satisfactory? Was it helpful? Was it healing? Was it meaningful? Did it advance reconciliation as they understand it? This collection does not articulate these responses per se, but it does discuss the historical, political, and religious contexts in which they are embedded. This diverse collection of analyses of Pope Francis's visit in 2022, having the fundamental aim of being attendant to survivors' experience of the visit, offers both critical and receptive perspectives of the visit itself as well as hope for the future.

In Catholic theology, pilgrimage evokes not only the ideas of journey and an awareness of faith but also the ideas of sin and grace. In identifying himself as a penitential pilgrim, Pope Francis acknowledged that he, as the leader of the global Roman Catholic Church, was living with and atoning for the sins committed by the church in the centuries since its arrival on Turtle Island. The image of the walk alone captures the solitude characteristic of sin and atonement, and the image of walking together captures the communal possibility of a future of grace and hope. The dynamic tension between these images invokes the reality that the journey is in its infancy and that there are many generations ahead who will be needed to enact both repentance and reconciliation.

As the authors note, the initial responses to Pope Francis's various apologies, both in Rome and on Indigenous lands, were mixed. Recounting these responses here would be redundant, but noting some key themes discussed by the authors is helpful. First, a number of the authors, notably Donald Bolen and Christine Jamieson, recall that Pope Francis's commitment to a "culture of encounter" was evident in his individual engagement with the Indian residential and day school survivors and their families. Whereas Bolen effectively outlines a possible action plan for the Catholic Church in Canada, Jamieson identifies a contrast between Pope Francis's personal engagement with the people he met and the hierarchical and somewhat tone-deaf organization of the two public Masses. This contrast perhaps signals the tensions that remain between the desire for reconciliation among all participants and the colonial barriers to its actualization. A culture of encounter calls for personal engagement as a means of reconciliation – that is, for a literal and metaphorical pilgrimage, or walking together. Pope Francis's awareness of this call was evident in the fact that he listened to and heard the accounts of Indigenous Peoples both in Rome and in Canada. Yet the distance placed between him and the elder's and survivors in the most public settings clearly detracted from the overall apologies. As the title of this collection notes, the journey presses on.

Annie Selak and Jeremy M. Bergen undertake ecclesiological analyses of the apologies both in light of the specific Catholic context (Selak) and in light of the broader Christian context (Bergen). Both Selak and Bergen note the missteps of Pope Francis's apologies and their steps forward. Noting Pope Francis's omission of the Doctrine of Discovery from his apologies and his gradual movement toward more specific and personal apologies between the time of the Indigenous delegation's visit to Rome and the time of his arrival on Indigenous soil, we must acknowledge, once again, that we are embarking on the mere beginning of the journey of atonement and reconciliation.

When Bergen takes up the petitions of Pope Francis for forgiveness, along with other such ecclesial or national petitions, he touches on the contentious practice of begging forgiveness within an apology. Again, the disparity of power here between the colonizers and the colonized supposes that the apology itself reactivates colonial imbalances and puts the onus on the colonized to facilitate reconciliation, perhaps prematurely. In an ecclesial context, we see the reiteration of a hierarchical disconnection from the historical dynamic of colonization.

Timothy Harvie also identifies the vestiges of colonialism in his close look at the Maskwacis and Lac Ste Anne visits, particularly in relation to the land. He notes the intrinsic Indigenous connection to the land in the context of the history of settler colonization of both the land and the peoples. Here, he notes Pope Francis's awareness of Indigenous identity connected with land while also noting the pope's move away from the actual land on which he stood in favour of a metaphorical relation to the biblical lands so powerful in the Jewish and Christian stories. In so doing, Harvie takes seriously the call for a papal apology on Indigenous soil and recognizes the colonial displacement of the lands that arises within the Christian identity. Appreciative of Pope Francis's apologetic gesture, he still recognizes the limitations of an apology that itself returns to the colonizers' story.

Métis scholar Chantal Fiola is an expert on the current and historical spiritual and ceremonial practices of various Métis communities. Fiola critiques the ongoing conflation of Catholic-Métis identity, as assumed by official Métis organizations and leaders. Fiola situates these dynamics within the church's role both in the initial colonization of Indigenous Peoples and in the ongoing unfolding of truth and reconciliation on Indigenous lands. Her calls for action from the Catholic Church reflect an understanding of apologies that have fallen short of many people's hopes, and she calls for an orientation to a future more amenable to Métis, First Nations, and Inuit peoples.

In their exploration of Pope Francis's penitential pilgrimage, Niigaanwewidam Sinclair and Darren Dias identify key themes and moments of his visit. Noting the initial *Calls to Action* (2015) of the Truth and Reconciliation Commission of Canada and the visit of the Indigenous delegation to Rome in the spring of 2022, Sinclair and Dias move beyond naming the suffering generated by colonization to consider the beginnings of reconciliation in the present and the hope for the future, which is to be found particularly in Indigenous youth. Together, they name the concrete steps toward a future more squarely focused on the shared humanity and dignity of Indigenous people globally. Like Timothy Harvie, they view the land as a spiritual home to Indigenous Peoples and view its reclamation – in material and spiritual terms – as necessary to decolonization. Although they recognize the numerous failings and missteps of Pope Francis's pilgrimage, they conclude that the journey toward healing and reconciliation has begun.

A key issue identified both during and immediately following Pope Francis's visit was his failure to repudiate the Doctrine of Discovery, the collective legal and political policies of assimilation and oppression stemming from medieval papal bulls that granted "conquering" nations primacy over "discovered" vacant lands (*terra nullius*). The papal decrees justified political and legal dispossession of Indigenous Peoples on Turtle Island, effecting unconscionable affliction among them.

The authors in this volume express diverse perceptions both of this omission during Pope Francis's time in Canada and of the subsequent release on 30 March 2023 of a joint statement from the Vatican's Dicasteries for Culture and Education and for Promoting Integral Human Development repudiating the concepts found within the documents and the ensuing use of the concepts to oppress and colonize Indigenous persons globally.[2] Some are wary of the repudiation and would have preferred a revocation or rescindment; some consider it to have been late but not without merit; some laud its place in the ongoing journey of reconciliation; and some see it as Pope Francis's delivery on the promise made while in Canada that a document of this sort would be forthcoming from the Vatican. How the repudiation will fit within the larger project of truth and reconciliation is yet to be seen.

Because the repudiation strongly recognizes the full personhood and dignity of every person and rejects any policies, teachings, or laws that deny them to all persons, it sits in line with the United Nations Declaration on the Rights of Indigenous Peoples (2007).[3] This repudiation is closely tied to the naming of genocide in the colonizing and oppressive practices of the churches and the Canadian government. While on the ground in Canada, Pope Francis did not name these practices of the church and governments as cultural genocide or as genocide generally. This omission was widely noted in Canada. On the return flight to Rome, when pressed by Canadian Press journalist Brittany Hobson, an Anishinaabe of Long Plain First Nation in Manitoba, the pope replied:

> It's true, I didn't use the word because it didn't come to my mind, but I described the genocide and asked for forgiveness, pardon for this activity that is genocidal. For example, I condemned this too: taking away children, changing culture, changing mentality, changing traditions, changing a race, let's put it that way, an entire culture.

> Yes, genocide is a technical word. I didn't use it because it didn't come to my mind. But I described it as true, yes, it was genocide … You go ahead and say that I said yes, it was genocide.[4]

This unscripted moment had tremendous and unforeseen consequences. Despite the many instances of missed communication, the use of the term "genocide" by Pope Francis enabled Indigenous commentators – even secular critics – to receive his visit retroactively with greater hospitality. Because Indigenous groups and leaders had long urged the Canadian government and public at large to accept that the process of colonization of Canada, including the residential schools, was a genocide, the pope's recognition of this fact was a moment of gratifying and surprising solidarity. When the House of Commons resumed its meetings in the fall after the papal visit, Winnipeg Centre's member of Parliament, Leah Gazan, was able to draw on the pope's acknowledgment in her motion: "That in the opinion of the House, this government must recognize what happened in Canada's Indian residential schools as genocide, as acknowledged by Pope Francis and in accordance with article II of the United Nations Convention on the Prevention and Punishment of the Crime of Genocide."[5]

Gazan's motion passed with unanimous consent in the House of Commons in October 2022. This motion had failed to pass in June 2021. Again, this unscripted moment was received differently among this volume's authors. But Pope Francis's willingness to clearly apply the term "genocide" to the conduct of the Indian residential schools when asked explicitly to do so was generally perceived as an indication of his acknowledgment of and repentance for the church's oppressive history in Canada. That the pope spoke the word itself also seemed powerful on the national stage.

Pope Francis's culture of encounter was tangible in his capacity to listen and respond to the suffering of generations of peoples during the visit. It was no small thing for survivors and their families of Indian residential and day schools to have the leader of the Catholic Church, the perpetrator of abuse and oppression, acknowledge their experiences and name them as the survivors themselves have done. The intricacies and implications of the pope's statement will play out over time, but we can say that naming genocide was a vital step in the journey toward reconciliation.

Returning to the title of this collection, *The Journey Presses On: Pope Francis's Apology to Residential School Survivors in Canada*, we emphasize that the overarching conclusion is a recognition of the long walk ahead to reconciliation. Although the journey is a long one, we believe that the elders – especially the survivors and the late Pope Francis himself – have set us on a good way.

NOTES

1 Pope Francis, "Angelus," 17 July 2022, https://www.vatican.va/content/francesco/en/angelus/2022/documents/20220717-angelus.html.

2 Holy See Press Office, "Joint Statement of the Dicasteries for Culture and Education and for Promoting Integral Human Development on the 'Doctrine of Discovery,'" 30 March 2023, https://press.vatican.va/content/salastampa/it/bollettino/pubblico/2023/03/30/0238/00515.html.

3 United Nations General Assembly, United Nations Declaration on the Rights of Indigenous Peoples (2007), https://www.un.org/development/desa/indigenouspeoples/wp-content/uploads/sites/19/2018/11/UNDRIP_E_web.pdf.

4 Pope Francis, "Press Conference on the Return Flight to Rome," 29 July 2022, https://www.vatican.va/content/francesco/en/speeches/2022/july/documents/20220729-voloritorno-canada.html.

5 Canada, *House of Commons Debates*, 44th Parliament, 1st Session, vol. 151, no. 119, 27 October 2022, 8966, https://www.ourcommons.ca/documentviewer/en/44-1/house/sitting-119/hansard.

Contributors

JANE BARTER (she/her) is professor of religion and culture at the University of Winnipeg. She holds a doctorate from the University of St Michael's College. Barter is the author of *Theopolitics and the Era of the Witness* (2025).

JEREMY M. BERGEN is associate professor of religious studies and theological studies at Conrad Grebel University College, University of Waterloo. Dr Bergen teaches and writes in the area of contemporary Christian theology. His research interests include church apologies for historical wrongs, martyrdom, ecclesiology, ecumenism, the doctrine of the Holy Spirit, and contemporary Mennonite theology. In his book *Ecclesial Repentance: The Churches Confront Their Sinful Pasts* (2011), he analyzes over one hundred instances of churches apologizing for historical wrongs and proposes a theological framework for understanding this relatively new practice. He is completing a book tentatively titled *Christian Martyrdom and the Unity of the Church*. Dr Bergen was the director of theological studies at Conrad Grebel from 2014 to 2021. He has served as director of the Toronto Mennonite Theological Centre and as editor of *The Conrad Grebel Review*, and he was president of the Canadian Theological Society from 2016 to 2017.

DONALD BOLEN has been the archbishop of the Catholic Archdiocese of Regina, Saskatchewan, since 2016.

DARREN DIAS, OP, PhD, is the executive director of the Toronto School of Theology and an associate professor of systematic theology at the University of St Michael's College. His areas of interest include Trinitarian theology, pneumatology, interreligious relations, and methodology. His recent publications include "Hard Sayings: New Questions for a Pilgrim Church" (2023), "Lonergan and Freire: An Initial Conversation" (2023), "Paulo Freire and Pope Francis on Dialogue: An Anticolonial Interpretation" (2022), and "Trinity, Elemental Meaning and Psychic Conversion: A Pastoral Consideration" (2022). In 2019, Dr Dias was appointed to the Canadian Conference of Catholic Bishops–Canadian Council of Imams Working Group, and from 2021 to 2022 he was a member of the theological group formed by the Vatican's Dicastery for Human Integral Formation to conduct the research project *Doing Theology from the Existential Peripheries* (2022). He has been the recipient of research awards from the Social Sciences and Humanities Research Council of Canada, the American Academy of Religion, and the Templeton Foundation, and he currently serves as the chair of the Lonergan Research Institute Board.

CHANTAL FIOLA is Michif (Red River Métis) with family from St Laurent, Ste Geneviève, and Ste Anne, Manitoba, and she is a registered citizen of the Manitoba Métis Federation. Dr Fiola is the associate vice-president of the Office of Indigenous Engagement at the University of Winnipeg, where she maintains an appointment as an associate professor in the Department of Urban and Inner-City Studies and was the Distinguished Indigenous Scholar's Chair from 2021 to 2024. Dr Fiola's award-winning work includes her second book, *Returning to Ceremony:*

Spirituality in Manitoba Métis Communities (2021). Currently, she is the project director on the three-year study "Expressions of Métis Spirituality and Religion across the Homeland," funded by the Social Sciences and Humanities Research Council of Canada. Dr Fiola is a member of the Circle of Editors for *Pawaatamihk* [Pah-WAH-tah-mik]*: Journal of Métis Thinkers*, served as a board member of Two-Spirit Manitoba from 2018 to 2025, and is a founding member of the Two-Spirit Michif Local of the Manitoba Métis Federation.

TIMOTHY HARVIE is professor of philosophy and ethics at St Mary's University in Calgary. Dr Harvie has authored, co-authored, or co-edited three books, including *Encountering Earth: Thinking Theologically with a More-Than-Human World* (2018), and is currently working on the forthcoming volume *Merleau-Ponty and the Politics of Transcendence: An Earthen Public Theology*. He has published several essays on Pope Francis, and his current research focuses on ecotheology and a liberative politics for the earth and its myriad inhabitants.

CHRISTINE JAMIESON is a member of the Boothroyd First Nation in British Columbia. Her paternal grandfather was a respected elder among the Boothroyd First Nation and among the people of the Nlaka'pamux Nation in the Fraser Canyon, British Columbia. Dr Jamieson earned a doctorate in Christian ethics from Saint Paul University in Ottawa. In 1998, she was hired in the Department of Theological Studies at Concordia University in Montreal, where she continues to teach courses in ethics, bioethics, Indigenous spirituality, and Lonergan studies.

DORIS M. KIESER is an associate professor and an associate academic dean at St Joseph's College, the Catholic College at the University of Alberta. She is the author of *Catholic Sexual Theology and Adolescent Girls: Embodied Flourishing* (2015), an adjunct associate professor at the John Dossetor Health Ethics Centre, and a counselling therapist with a small practice in Edmonton.

ANNIE SELAK (she/her/hers) is an expert in feminist theology and ecclesiology. Her first book, *The Wounded Church: Tending to the Harm within Catholicism* (2026), examines racism, sexism, and the clergy sex abuse crisis. Dr Selak is an instructor of feminist theology at Georgetown University and an associate editor of *Theological Studies: A Journal of Academic Theology*. She earned a doctorate in systematic theology at Boston College and a master of divinity degree at the Jesuit School of Theology at Berkeley.

NIIGAANWEWIDAM (NIIGAAN) SINCLAIR is Anishinaabe (St Peter's/Little Peguis) and a professor in the Faculty of Arts at the University of Manitoba, where he holds the Professorship in Indigenous Knowledge and Aesthetics and is currently head of the Department of Indigenous Studies. Dr Sinclair is also an award-winning writer, editor, and activist who was recently named to the "Power List" by *Maclean's* magazine as one of the most influential individuals in Canada. In 2018, he won Canadian columnist of the year at the National Newspaper Awards for his biweekly columns in the *Winnipeg Free Press* and is a featured member of the Friday "Power Panel" on the Canadian Broadcasting Corporation's television news program and podcast *Power & Politics*.

Index

Advancing Studies in Religion
Series editor: Sarah Wilkins-Laflamme

1 The al-Baqara Crescendo
Understanding the Qur an's Style, Narrative Structure, and Running Themes
Nevin Reda

2 Leaving Christianity
Changing Allegiances in Canada since 1945
Brian Clarke and Stuart Macdonald

3 Everyday Sacred
Religion in Contemporary Quebec
Edited by Hillary Kaell

4 Convergent Knowing
Christianity and Science in Conversation with a Suffering Creation
Simon Appolloni

5 Seeding Buddhism with Multiculturalism
The Transmission of Sri Lankan Buddhism in Toronto
D. Mitra Barua

6 The Subversive Evangelical
The Ironic Charisma of an Irreligious Megachurch
Peter J. Schuurman

7 The Public Work of Christmas
Difference and Belonging in Multicultural Societies
Edited by Pamela E. Klassen and Monique Scheer

8 Identities Under Construction
Religion, Gender, and Sexuality among Youth in Canada
Pamela Dickey Young and Heather Shipley

9 Prayer as Transgression?
The Social Relations of Prayer in Healthcare Settings
Sheryl Reimer-Kirkham, Sonya Sharma, Rachel Brown, and Melania Calestani

10 Relation and Resistance
Racialized Women, Religion, and Diaspora
Edited by Sailaja V. Krishnamurti and Becky R. Lee

11 Sacred as Secular
Secularization under Theocracy in Iran
Abdolmohammad Kazemipur

12 Under Siege
Islamophobia and the 9/11 Generation
Jasmin Zine

13 Sacred Cyberspaces
Catholicism, New Media, and the Religious Experience
Oren Golan and Michele Martini

14 Caught in the Current
British and Canadian Evangelicals in an Age of Self-Spirituality
Sam Reimer